100 GREATEST GUITAR INTROS

"Johnny B. Goode" (Chuck Berry) omitted due to copyright restriction.

ISBN 978-1-4803-9045-4

HAL•LEONARD® CORPORATION

7777 W. BLUEMOUND RD. P.O. BOX 13819 MILWAUKEE, WI 53213

Visit Hal Leonard Online at
www.halleonard.com

Table of Contents

Ain't Talkin' 'Bout Love

Words and Music by Edward Van Halen, Alex Van Halen, Michael Anthony and David Lee Roth

Tune down 1/2 step:
(low to high) Eb-Ab-Db-Gb-Bb-Eb

Moderately fast ♩ = 138

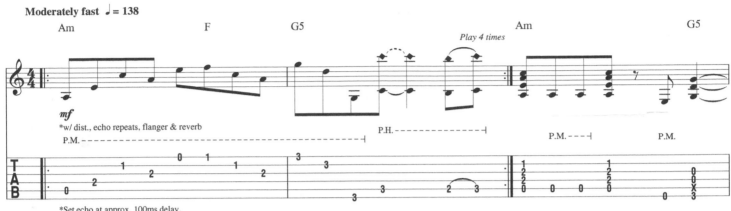

*w/ dist., echo repeats, flanger & reverb

*Set echo at approx. 100ms delay.
Set flanger for slow speed w/ regeneration sweep and moderate depth.

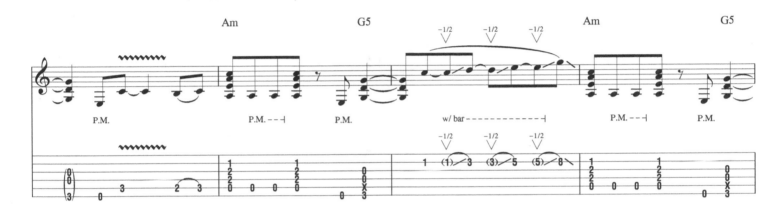

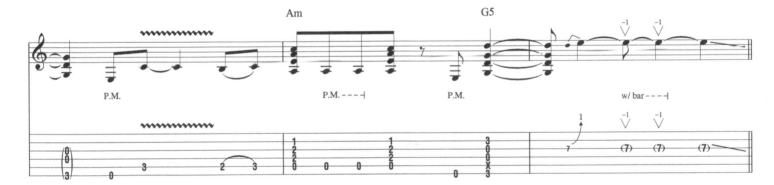

Artist: Van Halen

Album: *Van Halen*

Year: 1978

Guitarist: Edward Van Halen

Alive

Music by Stone Gossard
Lyric by Eddie Vedder

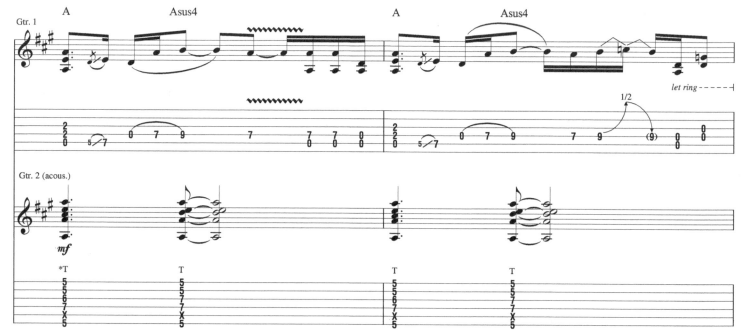

*T=Thumb on 6th str.

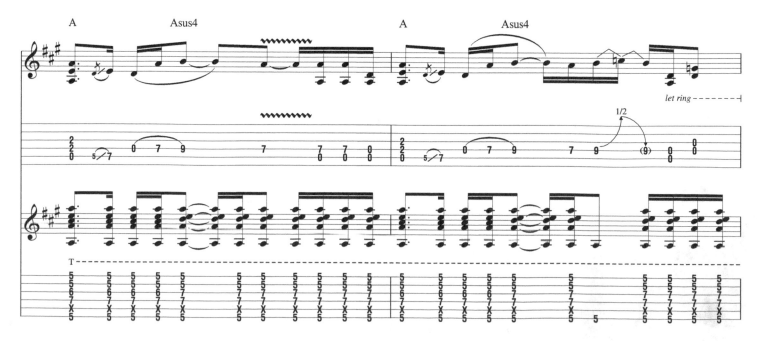

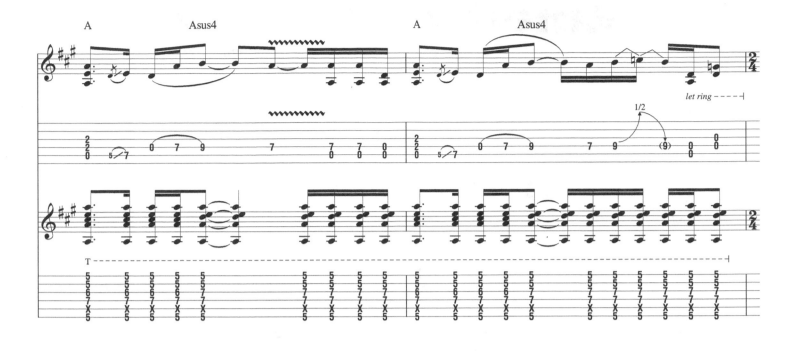

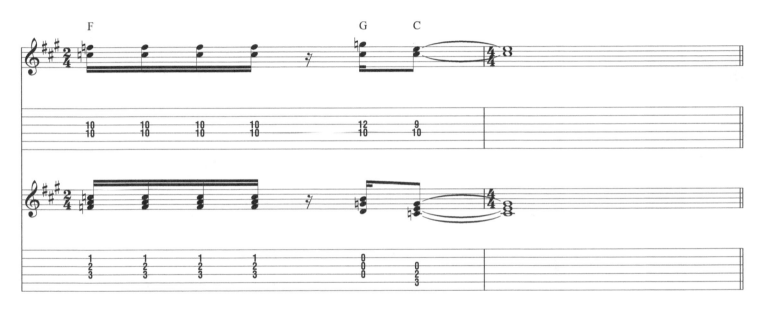

Artist: Pearl Jam

Album: *Ten*

Year: 1991

Guitarists: Mike McCready, Stone Gossard

American Woman

Written by Burton Cummings, Randy Bachman, Gary Peterson and Jim Kale

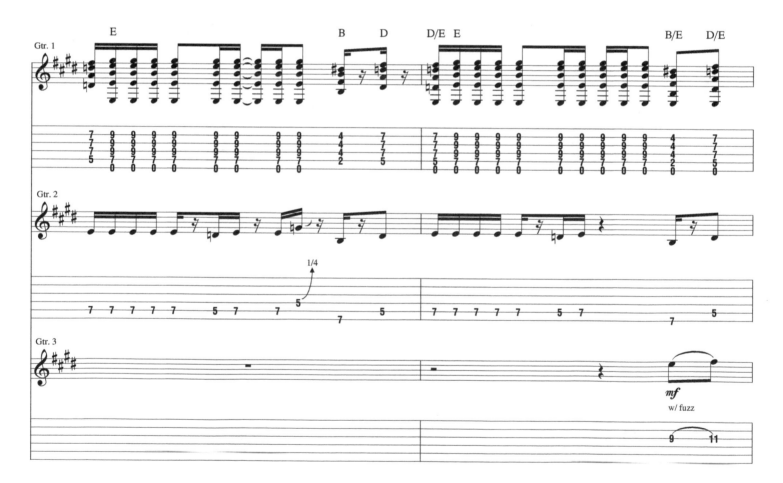

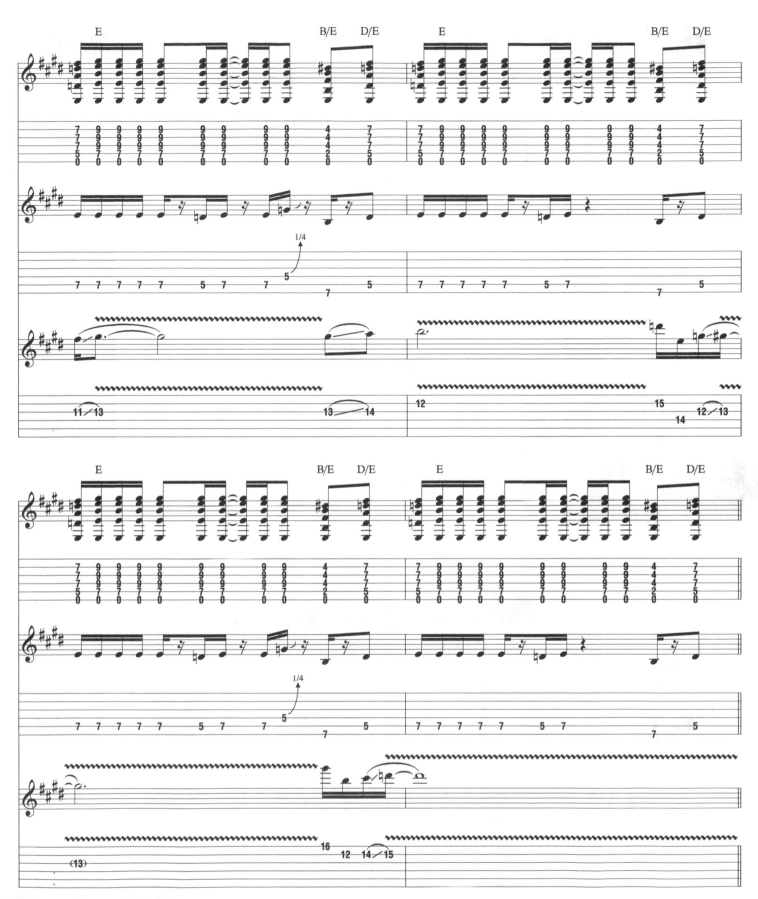

Artist: The Guess Who

Album: *American Woman*

Year: 1970

Guitarist: Randy Bachman

All Day and All of the Night

Words and Music by Ray Davies

Artist: The Kinks

Album: *Kinks-Size*

Year: 1964

Guitarists: Ray Davies, Dave Davies

All Right Now

Words and Music by Andy Fraser and Paul Rodgers

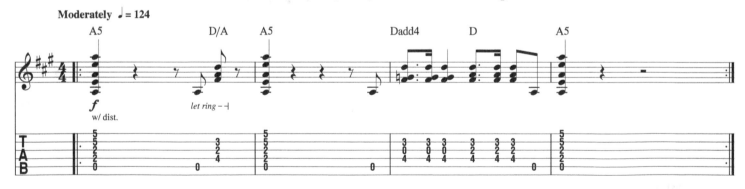

Artist: Free

Album: *Fire and Water*

Year: 1970

Guitarist: Paul Kossoff

Aqualung

Words and Music by Ian Anderson and Jennie Anderson

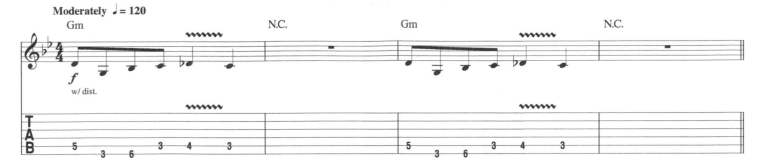

Artist: Jethro Tull

Album: *Aqualung*

Year: 1971

Guitarist: Martin Barre

Blackbird

Words and Music by John Lennon and Paul McCartney

*Strum upstemmed notes w/ index finger of picking hand
whenever more than one upstemmed note appears.

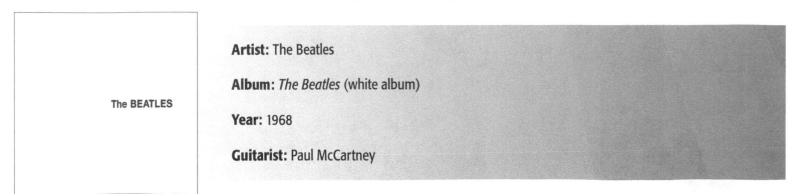

The BEATLES

Artist: The Beatles

Album: *The Beatles* (white album)

Year: 1968

Guitarist: Paul McCartney

Are You Gonna Go My Way

Words by Lenny Kravitz
Music by Lenny Kravitz and Craig Ross

Artist: Lenny Kravitz

Album: *Are You Gonna Go My Way*

Year: 1993

Guitarists: Lenny Kravitz, Craig Ross

Bad to the B--ne

Words and Music by George Thorogood

Artist: George Thorogood & the Destroyers

Album: *Bad to the Bone*

Year: 1982

Guitarist: George Thorogood

Barracuda

Words and Music by Nancy Wilson, Ann Wilson, Michael Derosier and Roger Fisher

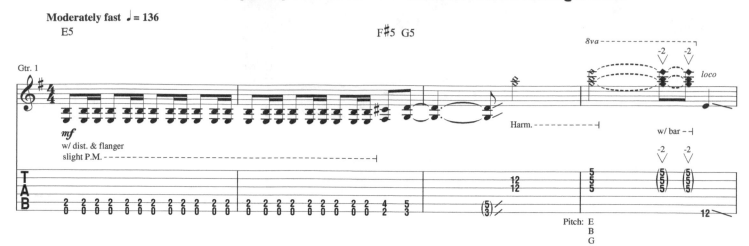

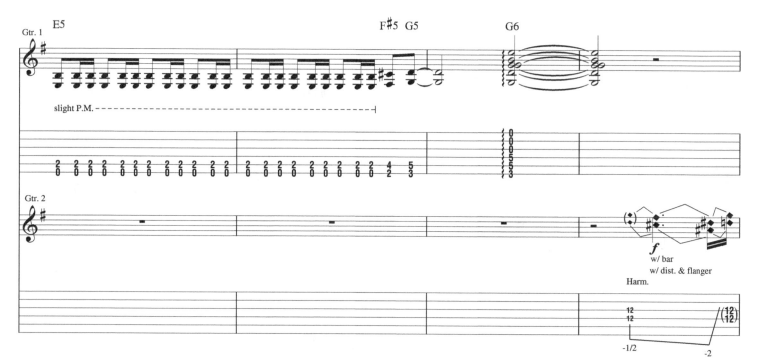

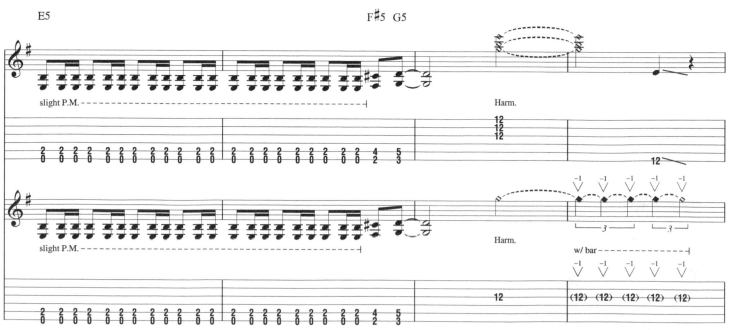

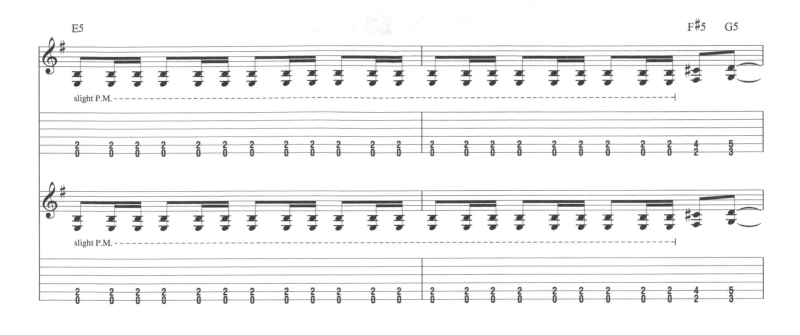

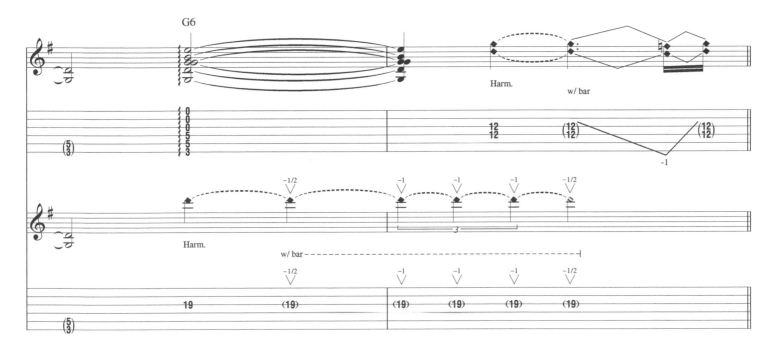

Artist: Heart

Album: *Little Queen*

Year: 1977

Guitarists: Nancy Wilson, Roger Fisher

Boom Boom

Words and Music by John Lee Hooker

Tune up 1/2 step:
(low to high) E#–A#–D#–G#–B#–E#

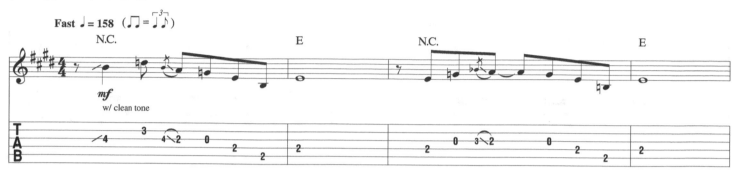

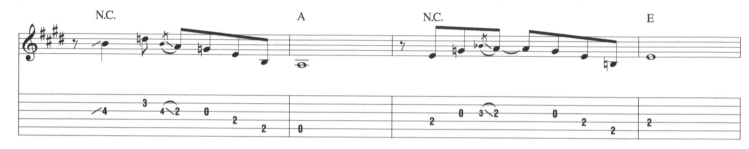

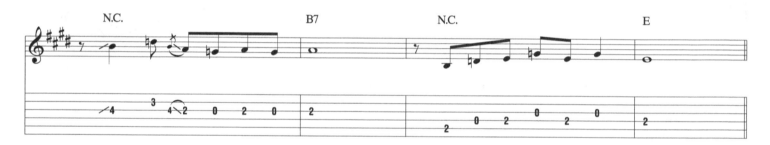

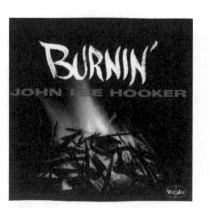

Artist: John Lee Hooker

Album: *Burnin'*

Year: 1962

Guitarists: John Lee Hooker, Larry Veeder

Brown Eyed Girl

Words and Music by Van Morrison

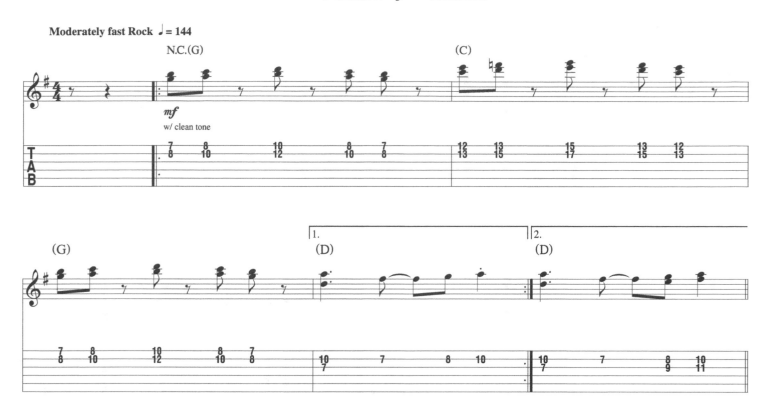

Artist: Van Morrison

Album: *Blowin' Your Mind!*

Year: 1967

Guitarists: Eric Gale, Hugh McCracken, Al Gorgoni

China Grove

Words and Music by Tom Johnston

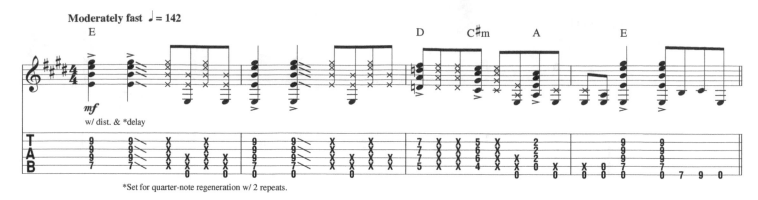

*Set for quarter-note regeneration w/ 2 repeats.

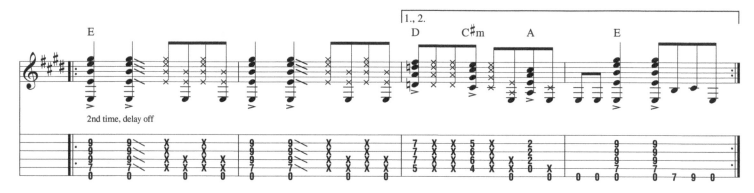

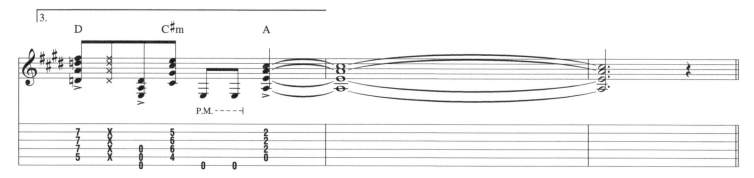

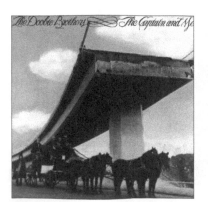

Artist: The Doobie Brothers

Album: *The Captain and Me*

Year: 1973

Guitarists: Tom Johnston, Patrick Simmons

Crazy Train

Words and Music by Ozzy Osbourne, Randy Rhoads and Bob Daisley

Moderately fast Rock ♩ = 138

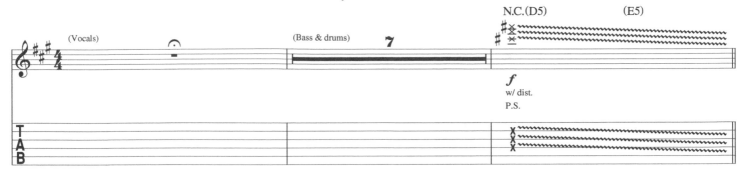

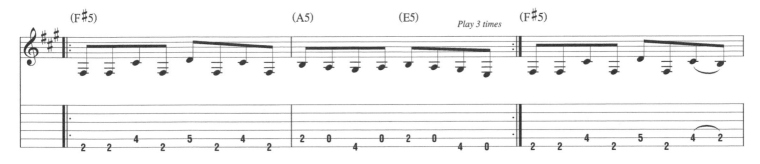

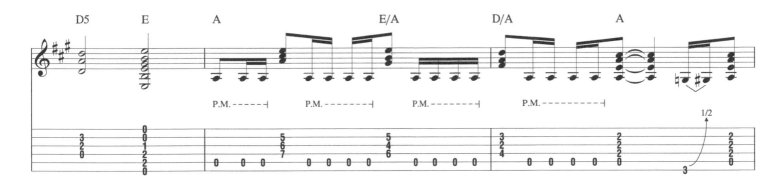

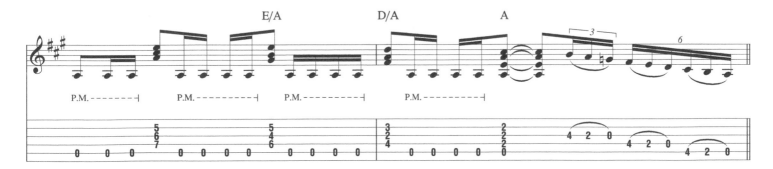

Artist: Ozzy Osbourne

Album: *Blizzard of Ozz*

Year: 1981

Guitarist: Randy Rhoads

Cliffs of Dover

By Eric Johnson

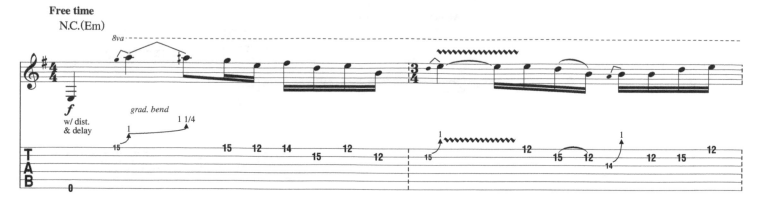

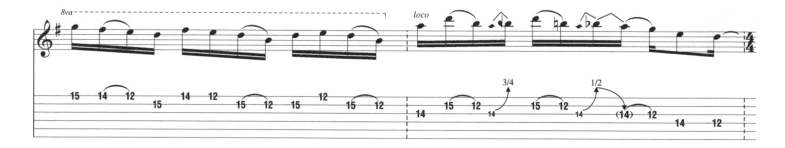

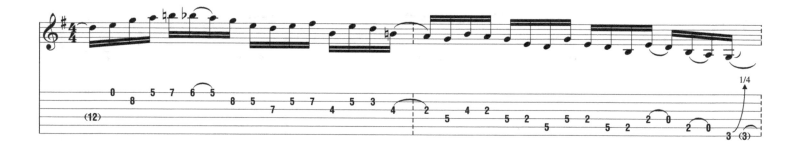

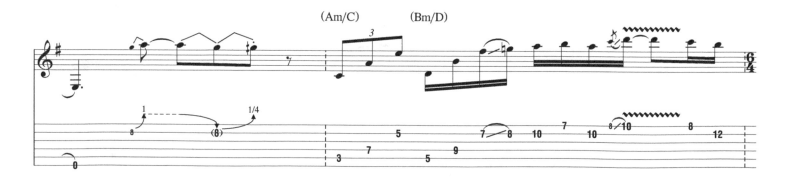

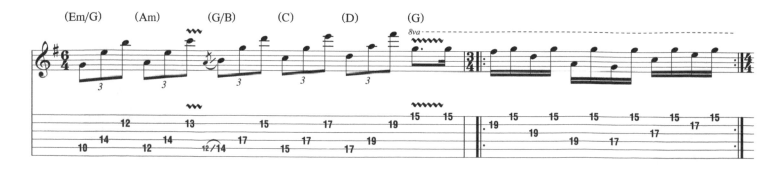

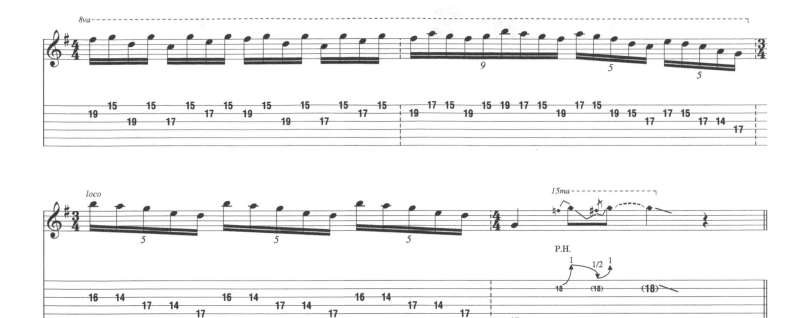

Artist: Eric Johnson

Album: *Ah Via Musicom*

Year: 1990

Guitarist: Eric Johnson

Cross Road Blues
(Crossroads)

Words and Music by Robert Johnson

Moderately fast Rock ♩ = 130

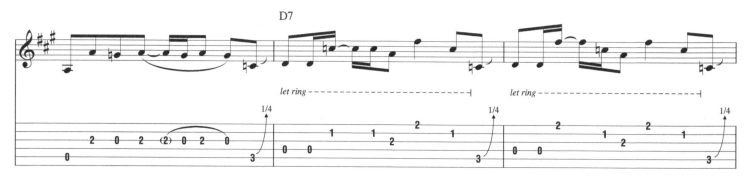

Artist: Cream

Album: *Wheels of Fire*

Year: 1968

Guitarist: Eric Clapton

Cult of Personality

Words and Music by Corey Glover, Manuel Skillings, William Calhoun and Vernon Reid

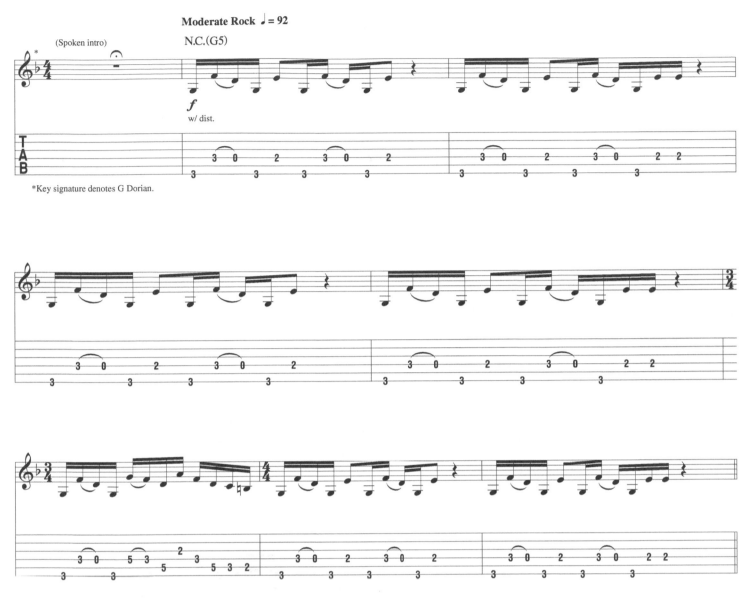

*Key signature denotes G Dorian.

Artist: *Living Colour*

Album: *Vivid*

Year: 1988

Guitarist: Vernon Reid

Day Tripper

Words and Music by John Lennon and Paul McCartney

Artist: The Beatles

Album: *Yesterday ...And Today*

Year: 1966

Guitarists: John Lennon, George Harrison

Dust in the Wind

Words and Music by Kerry Livgren

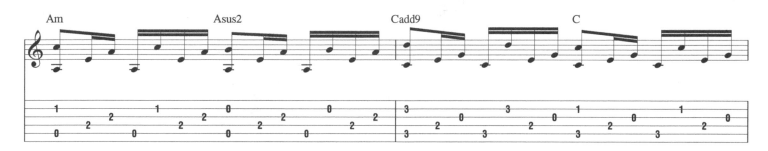

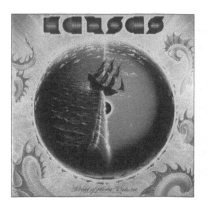

Artist: Kansas

Album: *Point of Know Return*

Year: 1977

Guitarists: Kerry Livgren, Richard Williams

Detroit Rock City

Words and Music by Paul Stanley and Bob Ezrin

Tune down 1/2 step:
(low to high) Eb-Ab-Db-Gb-Bb-Eb

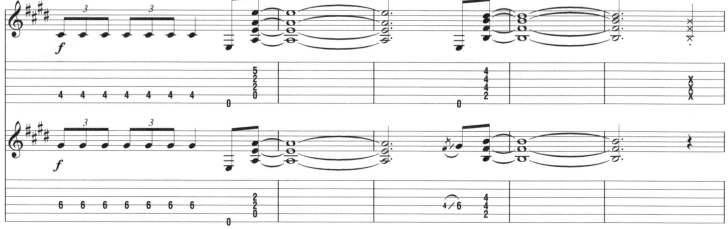

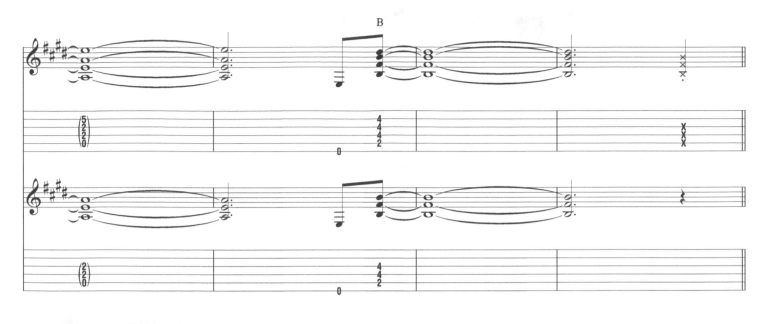

Artist: KISS

Album: *Destroyer*

Year: 1976

Guitarists: Paul Stanley, Ace Frehley

Don't Fear the Reaper

Words and Music by Donald Roeser

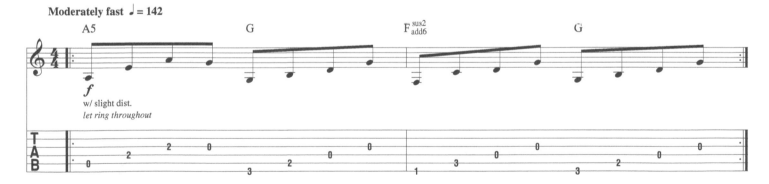

Artist: Blue Öyster Cult

Album: *Agents of Fortune*

Year: 1976

Guitarists: Donald "Buck Dharma" Roeser, Eric Bloom

Enter Sandman

Words and Music by James Hetfield, Lars Ulrich and Kirk Hammett

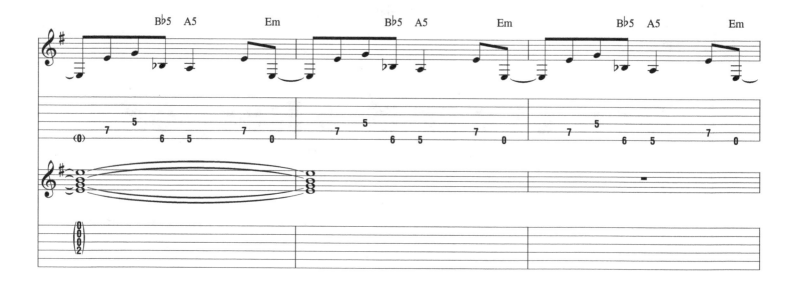

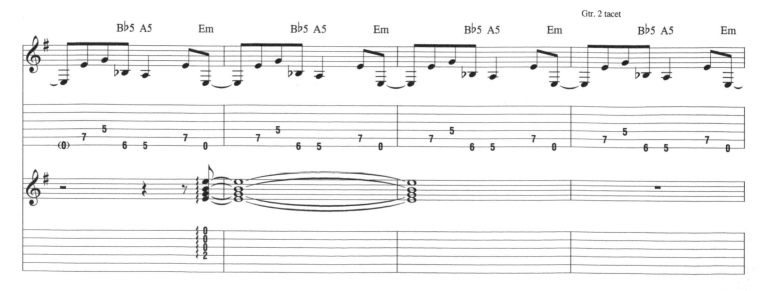

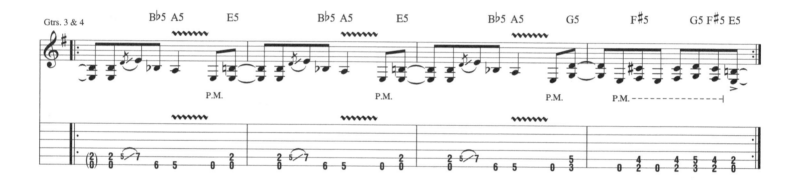

Artist: Metallica

Album: *Metallica* (black album)

Year: 1991

Guitarists: James Hetfield, Kirk Hammett

Fly Like an Eagle

Words and Music by Steve Miller

Artist: Steve Miller Band

Album: *Fly Like an Eagle*

Year: 1976

Guitarist: Steve Miller

Free Ride

Words and Music by Dan Hartman

Artist: Edgar Winter Group

Album: *They Only Come Out at Night*

Year: 1972

Guitarists: Ronnie Montrose, Rick Derringer

Fun, Fun, Fun

Words and Music by Brian Wilson and Mike Love

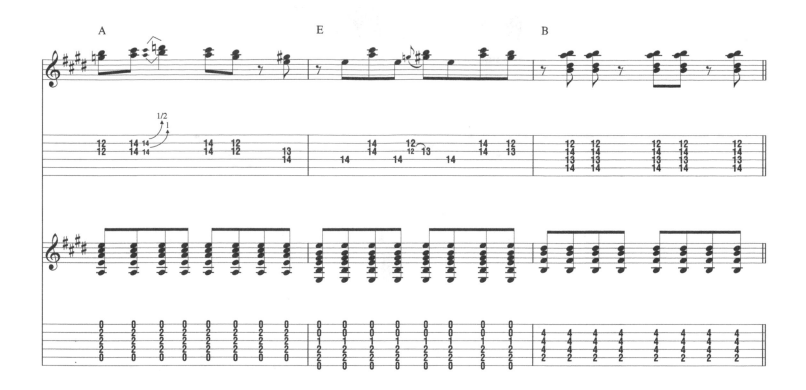

Artist: The Beach Boys

Album: *Shut Down Volume 2*

Year: 1964

Guitarists: Carl Wilson, Al Jardine

Funk #49

Words and Music by Joe Walsh, Dale Peters and James Fox

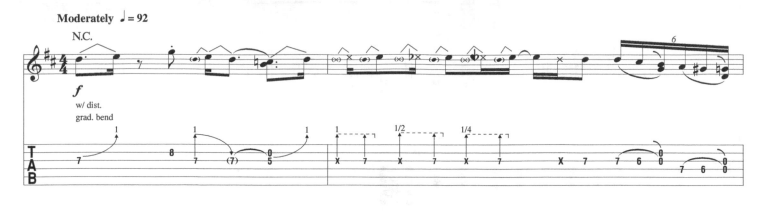

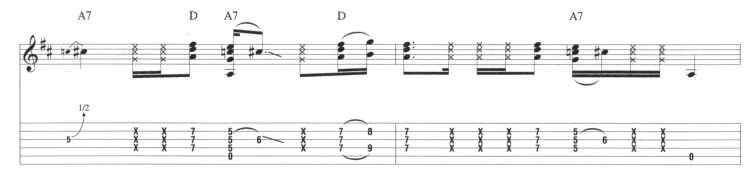

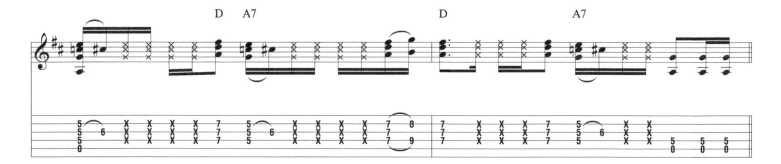

Artist: James Gang

Album: *Rides Again*

Year: 1970

Guitarists: Joe Walsh, Dale Peters

Heartbreaker

Words and Music by Jimmy Page, Robert Plant, John Paul Jones and John Bonham

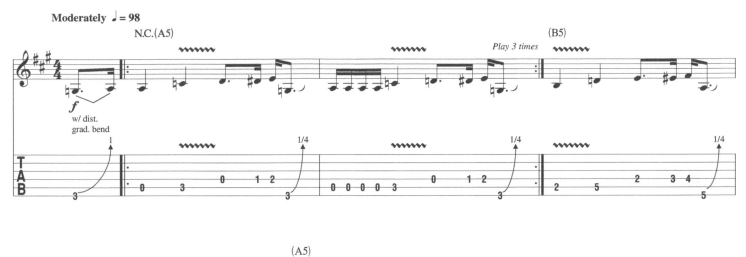

Artist: Led Zeppelin

Album: *Led Zeppelin II*

Year: 1969

Guitarist: Jimmy Page

Heaven

Words and Music by Henry Garza, Joey Garza and Ringo Garza

Tune down 1/2 step:
(low to high) Eb-Ab-Db-Gb-Bb-Eb

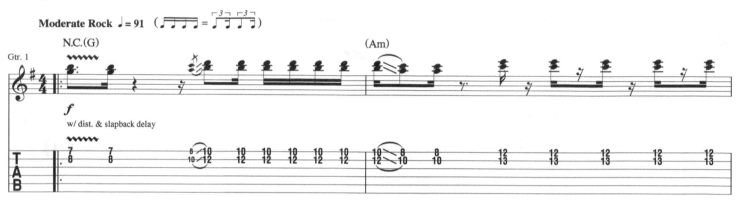

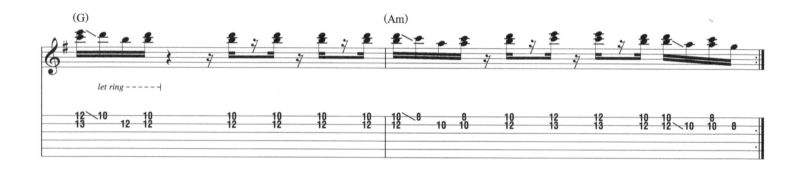

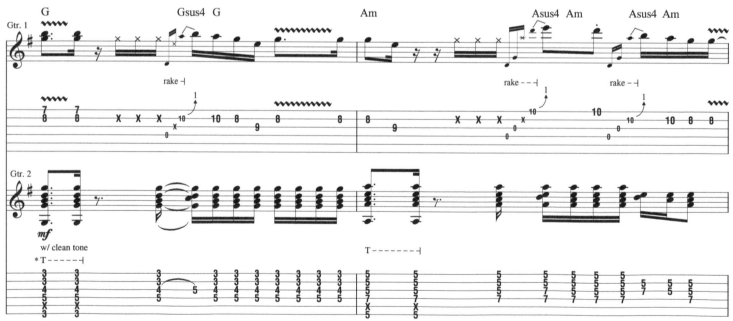

*T = Thumb on 6th string

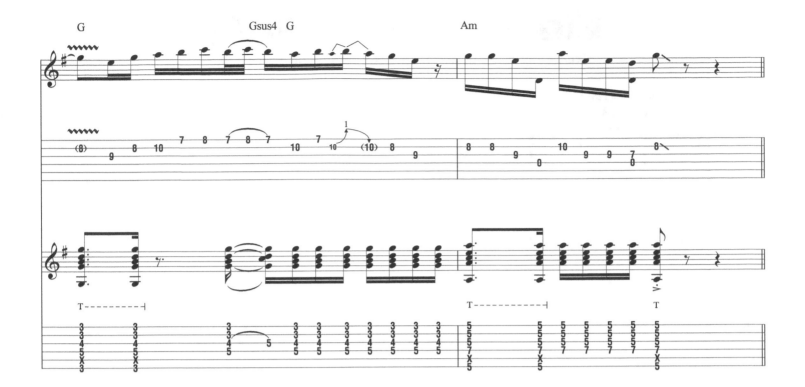

Artist: Los Lonely Boys

Album: *Los Lonely Boys*

Year: 2004

Guitarist: Henry Garza

Hold On Loosely

Words and Music by Jeff Carlisi, Don Barnes and Jim Peterik

Artist: 38 Special

Album: *Wild-Eyed Southern Boys*

Year: 1981

Guitarists: Jeff Carlisi, Don Barnes

The House of the Rising Sun

Words and Music by Alan Price

Artist: The Animals

Album: *The Animals*

Year: 1964

Guitarist: Hilton Valentine

Hotel California

Words and Music by Don Henley, Glenn Frey and Don Felder

Gtr. 1: Capo VII

*Symbols in parentheses represent chord names respective to capoed gtr.
Symbols above reflect actual sounding chords. Capoed fret is "0" in tab.

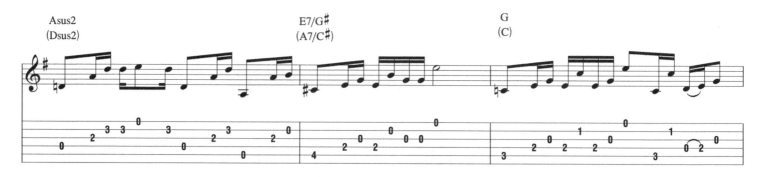

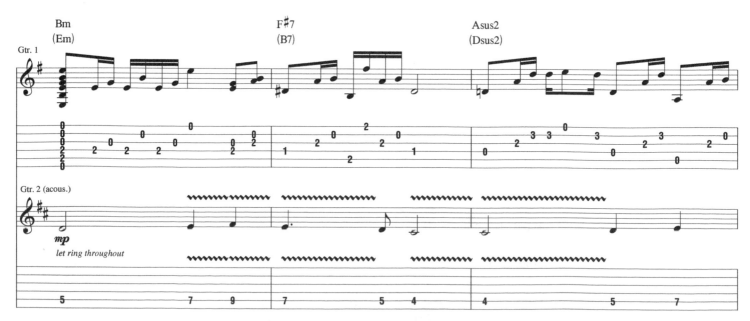

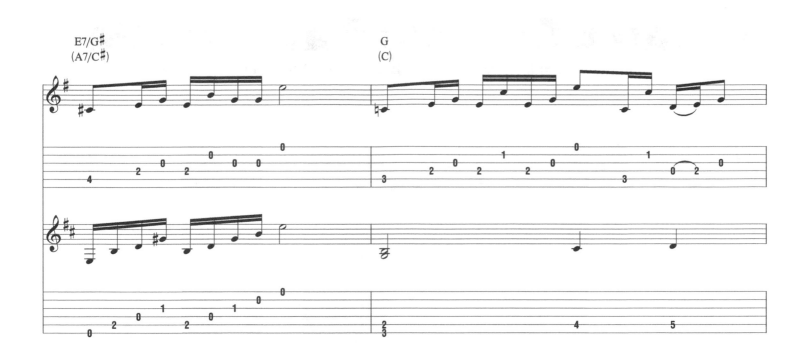

**T=Thumb on 6th string

Artist: Eagles

Album: *Hotel California*

Year: 1976

Guitarists: Don Felder, Joe Walsh, Glenn Frey

(I Can't Get No) Satisfaction

Words and Music by Mick Jagger and Keith Richards

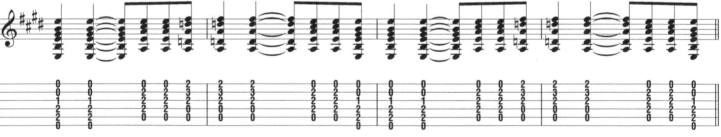

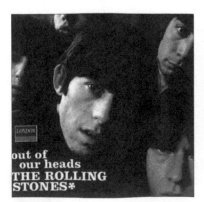

Artist: The Rolling Stones

Album: *Out of Our Heads*

Year: 1965

Guitarists: Keith Richards, Brian Jones

I Feel Fine

Words and Music by John Lennon and Paul McCartney

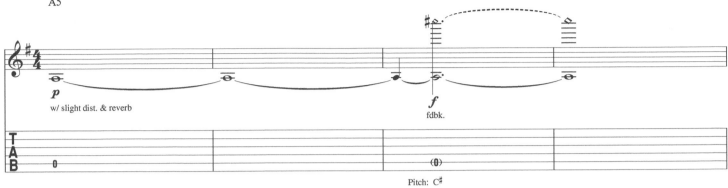

Artist: The Beatles

Album: *Beatles '65*

Year: 1964

Guitarists: John Lennon, George Harrison

Iron Man

Words and Music by Frank Iommi, John Osbourne, William Ward and Terence Butler

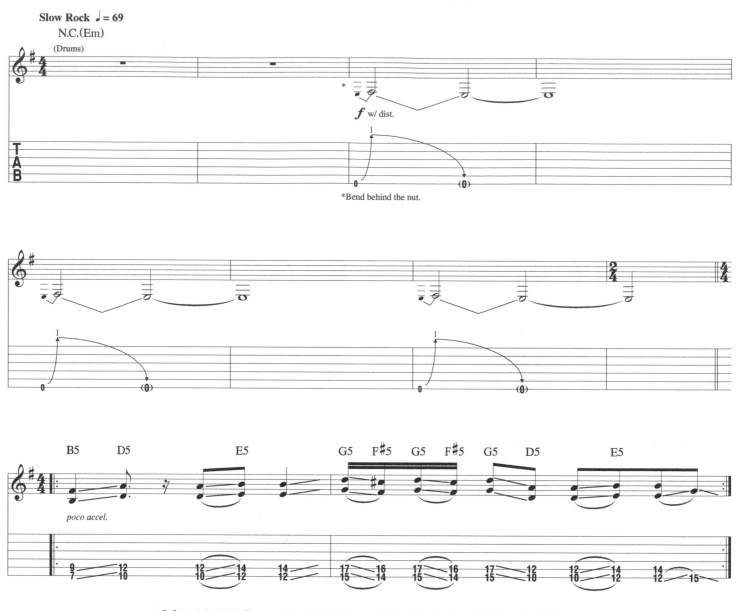

Artist: Black Sabbath

Album: *Paranoid*

Year: 1971

Guitarist: Tony Iommi

La Bamba

By Ritchie Valens

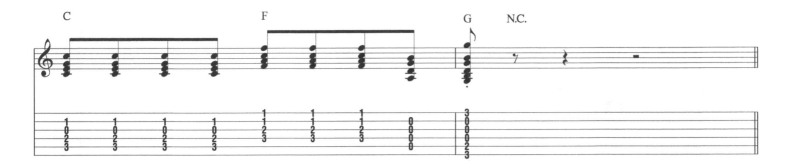

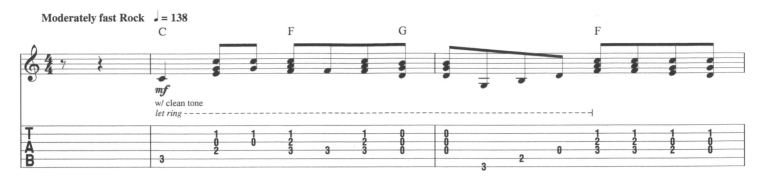

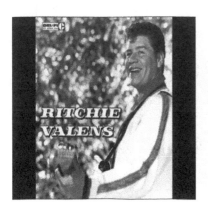

Artist: Ritchie Valens

Album: *Ritchie Valens*

Year: 1959

Guitarist: Ritchie Valens

La Grange

Words and Music by Billy F Gibbons, Dusty Hill and Frank Lee Beard

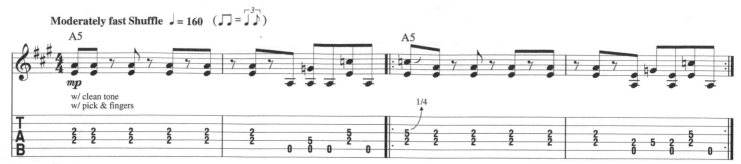

Artist: *ZZ Top*

Album: *Tres Hombres*

Year: 1973

Guitarist: Billy Gibbons

Layla

Words and Music by Eric Clapton and Jim Gordon

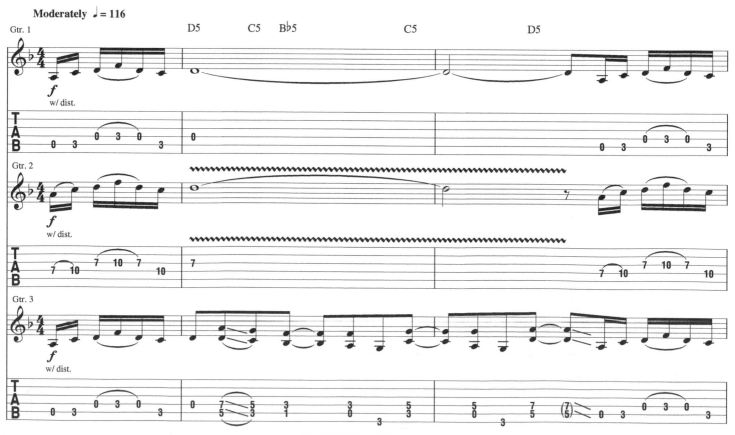

Artist: Derek and the Dominos

Album: *Layla and Other Assorted Love Songs*

Year: 1970

Guitarists: Eric Clapton, Duane Allman

Life in the Fast Lane

Words and Music by Don Henley, Glenn Frey and Joe Walsh

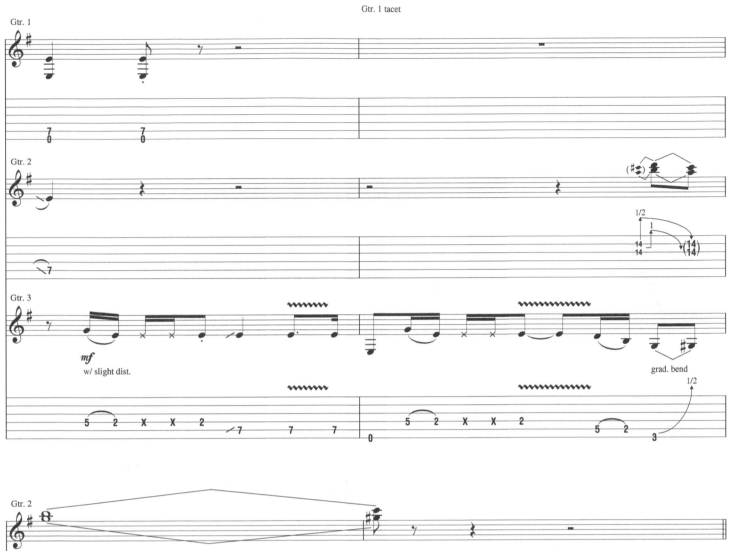

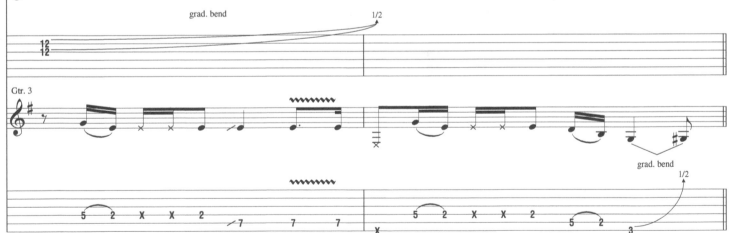

Artist: Eagles

Album: *Hotel California*

Year: 1976

Guitarists: Glenn Frey, Joe Walsh, Don Felder

Limelight

Words by Neil Peart
Music by Geddy Lee and Alex Lifeson

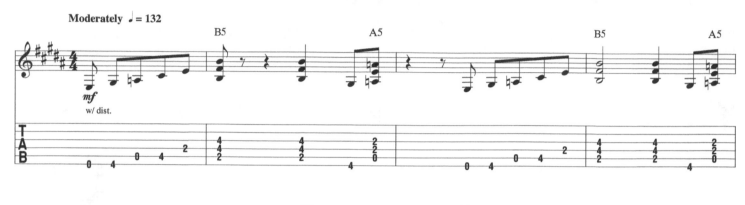

Artist: Rush

Album: *Moving Pictures*

Year: 1981

Guitarist: Alex Lifeson

Lonely Is the Night

Words and Music by Billy Squier

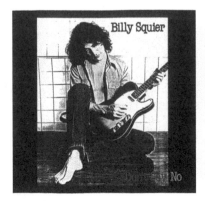

Artist: Billy Squier

Album: *Don't Say No*

Year: 1981

Guitarists: Billy Squier, Cary Sharaf

Long Cool Woman
(In a Black Dress)

Words and Music by Allan Clarke, Roger Cook and Roger Greenaway

Artist: The Hollies

Album: *Distant Light*

Year: 1971

Guitarists: Terry Sylvester, Allan Clarke, Tony Hicks

Love Song

Words and Music by Jeffrey Keith and Frank Hannon

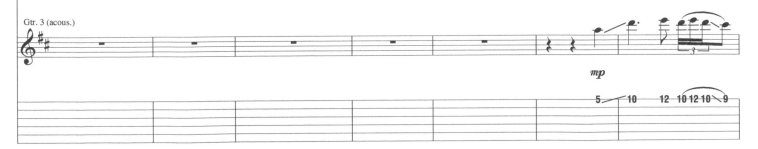

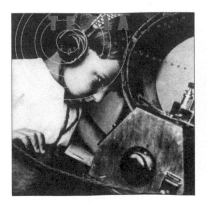

Artist: Tesla

Album: *The Great Radio Controversy*

Year: 1989

Guitarists: Frank Hannon, Tommy Skeoch

Mama, I'm Coming Home

Words and Music by Ozzy Osbourne and Zakk Wylde

Tune down 1/2 step:
(low to high) Eb-Ab-Db-Gb-Bb-Eb

Moderately slow ♩ = 69

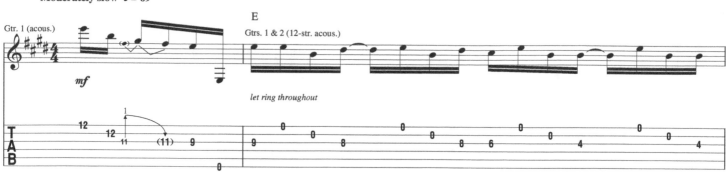

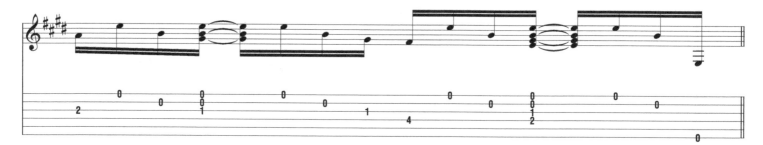

Artist: Ozzy Osbourne

Album: *No More Tears*

Year: 1991

Guitarist: Zakk Wylde

Message in a Bottle

Music and Lyrics by Sting

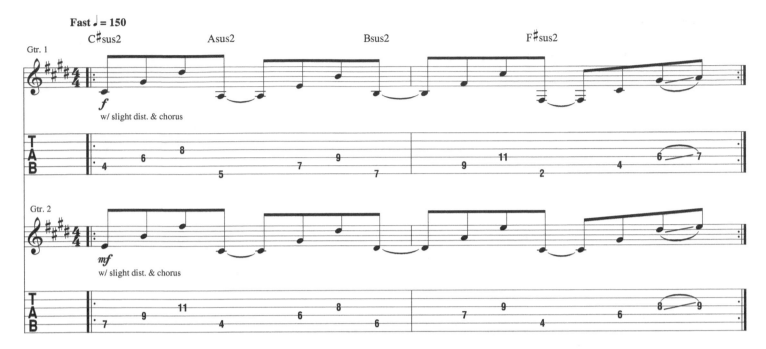

Artist: The Police

Album: *Regatta de Blanc*

Year: 1979

Guitarist: Andy Summers

Money for Nothing

Words and Music by Mark Knopfler and Sting

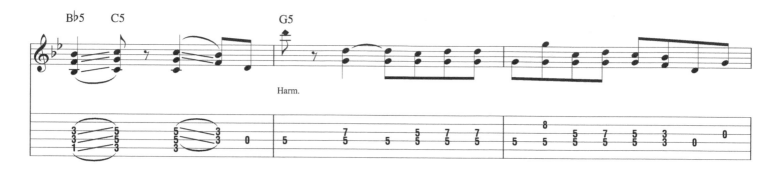

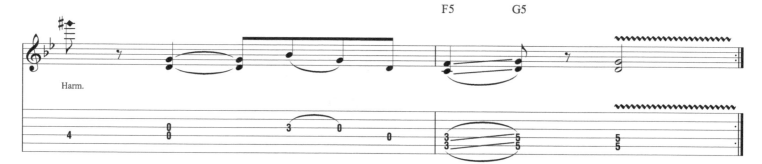

Artist: Dire Straits

Album: *Brothers in Arms*

Year: 1985

Guitarist: Mark Knopfler

More Than a Feeling

Words and Music by Tom Scholz

*Gtr. 1 (acous.); Gtr. 2 (12-str. acous.)

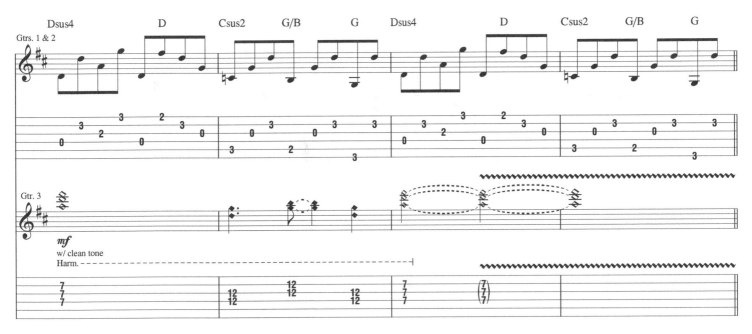

Artist: Boston

Album: *Boston*

Year: 1976

Guitarist: Tom Scholz

More Than Words

Words and Music by Nuno Bettencourt and Gary Cherone

Tune down 1/2 step:
(low to high) Eb-Ab-Db-Gb-Bb-Eb

Moderately slow ♩ = 96

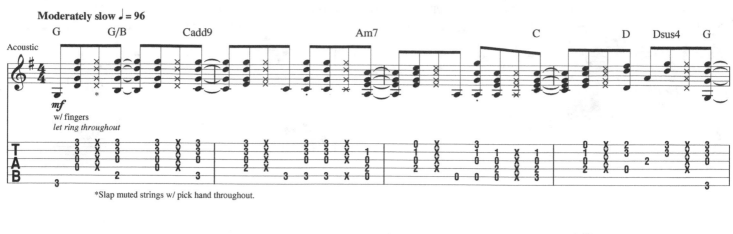

*Slap muted strings w/ pick hand throughout.

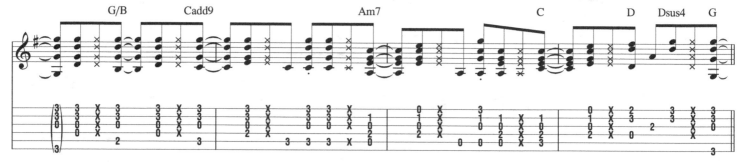

Artist: Extreme

Album: *Extreme II: Pornograffitti*

Year: 1990

Guitarist: Nuno Bettencourt

Mysterious Ways

Lyrics by Bono and The Edge
Music by U2

*Symbol in parentheses represents chord name respective to capoed guitars.
Symbol above reflects actual sounding chord (relative to detuning).
Capoed fret is "0" in tab.

Artist: U2

Album: *Achtung Baby*

Year: 1991

Guitarist: The Edge

Oh Well Part 1

Words and Music by Peter Green

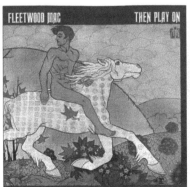

Artist: Fleetwood Mac

Album: *Then Play On*

Year: 1969

Guitarists: Peter Green, Danny Kirwan

Owner of a Lonely Heart

Words and Music by Trevor Rabin, Jon Anderson, Chris Squire and Trevor Horn

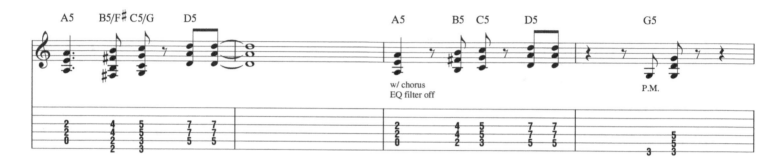

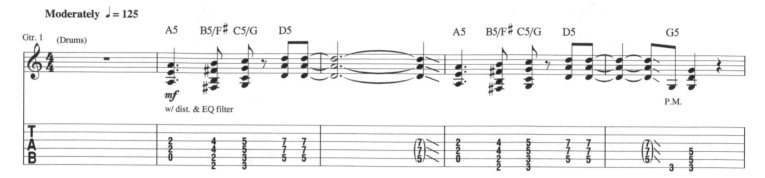

*Octaver set for 1 octave above.

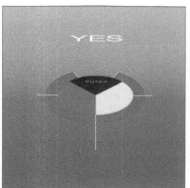

Artist: Yes

Album: *90125*

Year: 1983

Guitarist: Trevor Rabin

Paranoid

Words and Music by Anthony Iommi, John Osbourne, William Ward and Terence Butler

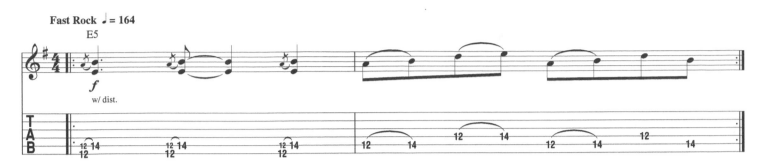

Artist: Black Sabbath

Album: *Paranoid*

Year: 1971

Guitarist: Tony Iommi

Plush

Words and Music by Scott Weiland, Dean DeLeo, Robert DeLeo and Eric Kretz

Artist: Stone Temple Pilots

Album: *Core*

Year: 1992

Guitarist: Dean DeLeo

Photograph

Words and Music by Joe Elliott, Steve Clark, Peter Willis, Richard Savage, Richard Allen and R.J. Lange

Artist: Def Leppard

Album: *Pyromania*

Year: 1983

Guitarists: Steve Clark, Phil Collen

Pride and Joy

Written by Stevie Ray Vaughan

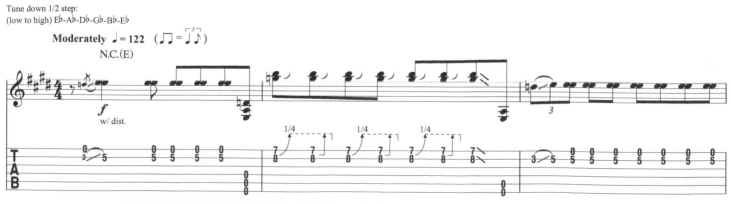

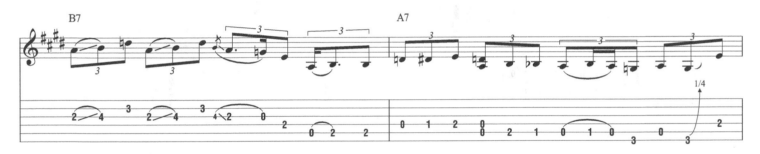

Artist: Stevie Ray Vaughan and Double Trouble

Album: *Texas Flood*

Year: 1983

Guitarist: Stevie Ray Vaughan

Pinball Wizard

Words and Music by Peter Townshend

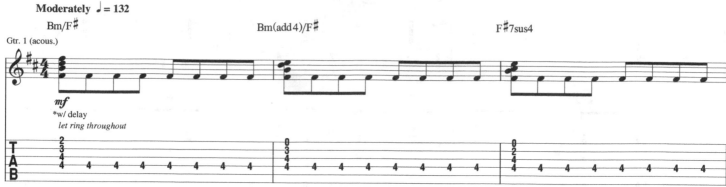

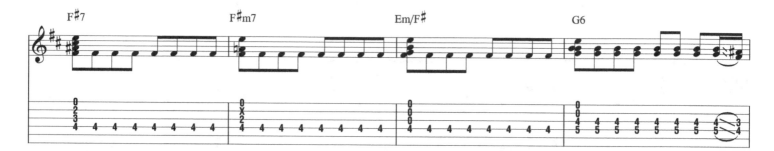

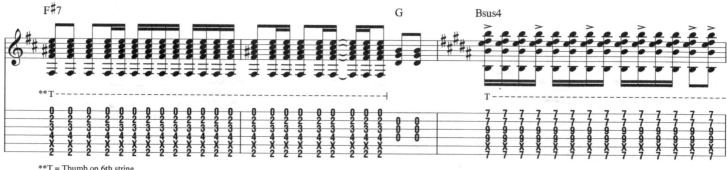

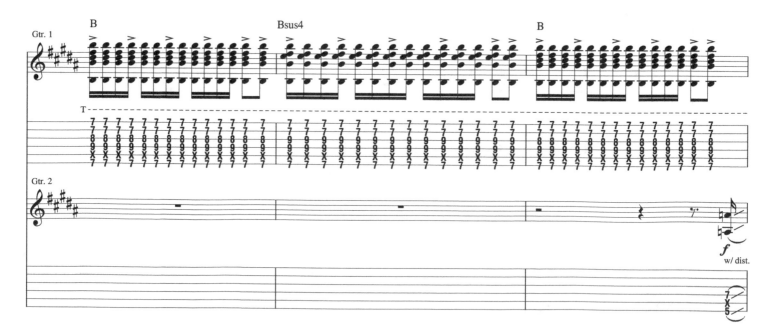

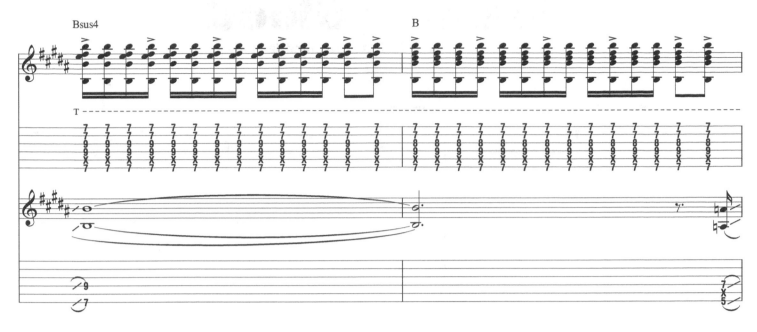

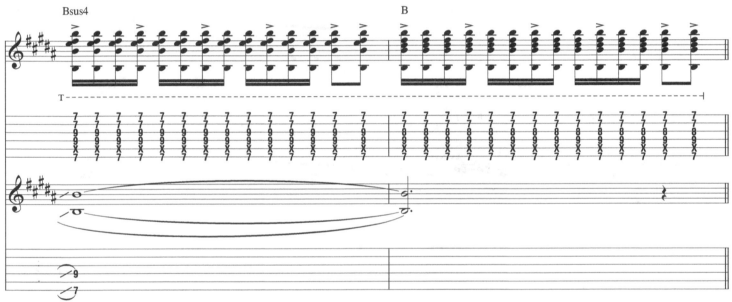

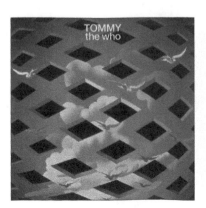

Artist: The Who

Album: *Tommy*

Year: 1969

Guitarist: Pete Townshend

Raining Blood

Words and Music by Jeff Hanneman and Kerry King

Tune down 1/2 step:
(low to high) Eb-Ab-Db-Gb-Bb-Eb

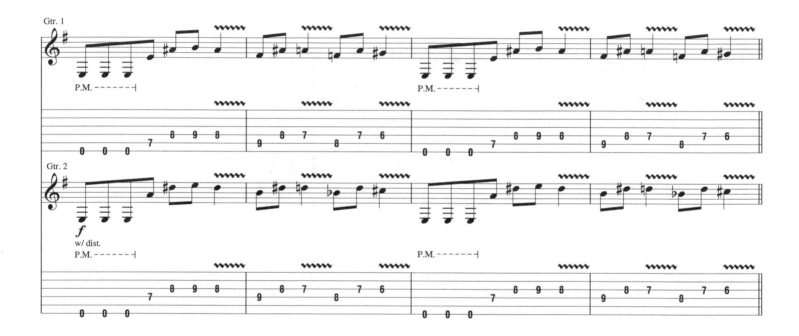

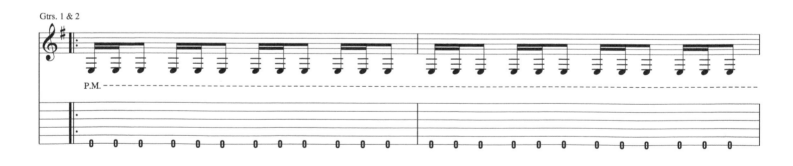

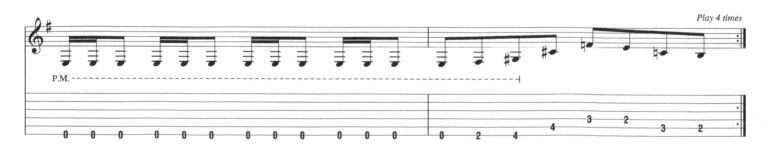

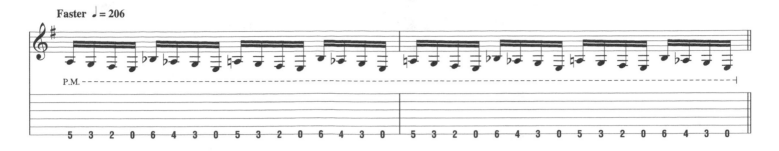

Artist: Slayer

Album: *Reign in Blood*

Year: 1986

Guitarists: Kerry King, Jeff Hanneman

Ramblin' Man

Words and Music by Dickey Betts

© 1973 (Renewed) UNICHAPPELL MUSIC INC. and FORREST RICHARD BETTS MUSIC
All Rights Administered by UNICHAPPELL MUSIC INC.
All Rights Reserved   Used by Permission

Artist: The Allman Brothers Band

Album: *Brothers and Sisters*

Year: 1973

Guitarists: Dickey Betts, Les Dudek

Rebel Yell

Words and Music by Billy Idol and Steve Stevens

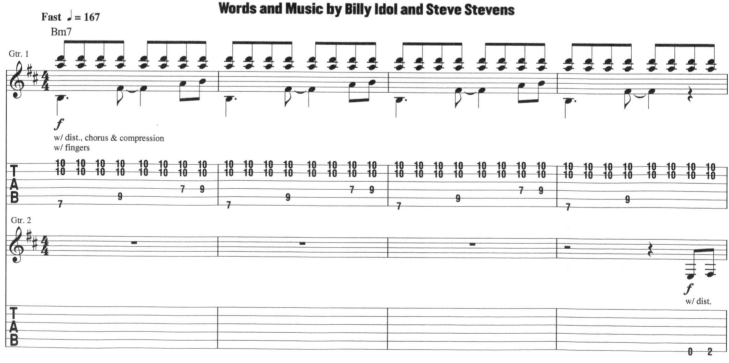

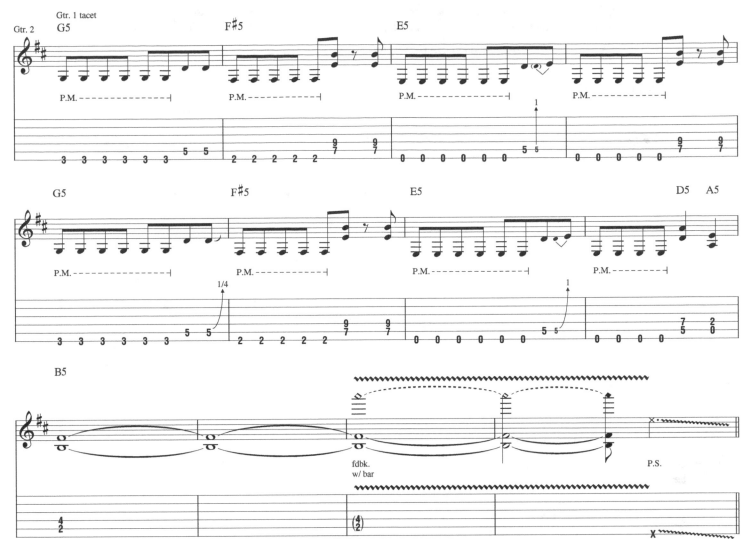

Artist: Billy Idol

Album: *Rebel Yell*

Year: 1984

Guitarist: Steve Stevens

Reeling in the Years

Words and Music by Walter Becker and Donald Fagen

Moderately fast ♩ = 138

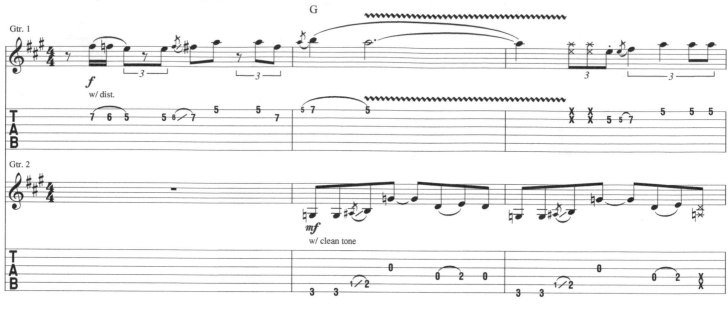

Artist: Steely Dan

Album: *Can't Buy a Thrill*

Year: 1973

Guitarists: Denny Dias, Jeff Baxter, Elliott Randall

Rebel, Rebel

Words and Music by David Bowie

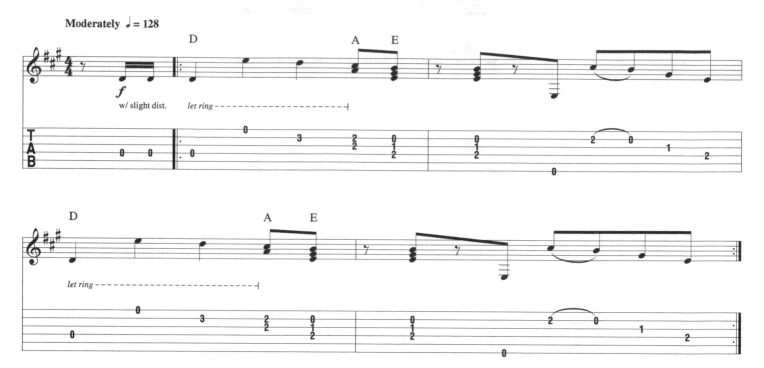

Artist: David Bowie

Album: *Diamond Dogs*

Year: 1974

Guitarist: David Bowie

Revolution

Words and Music by John Lennon and Paul McCartney

Tune up 1 step:
(low to high) F#-B-E-A-C#-F#

Moderately ♩ = 119

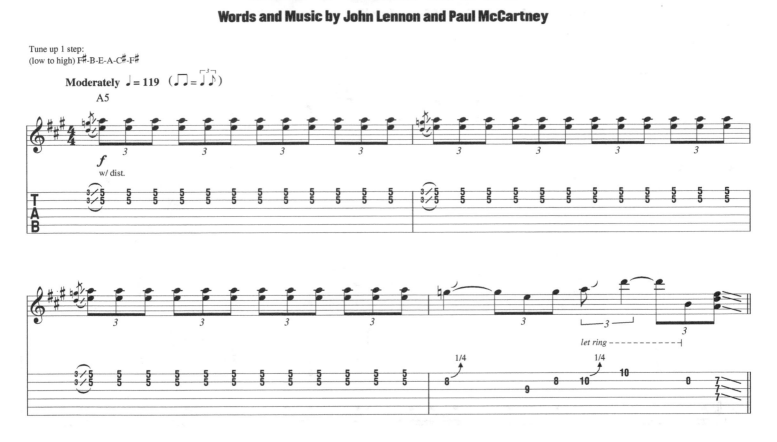

The BEATLES

Artist: The Beatles

Album: *The Beatles* (white album)

Year: 1968

Guitarists: John Lennon, George Harrison

Rock You Like a Hurricane

Words and Music by Rudolf Schenker, Klaus Meine and Herman Rarebell

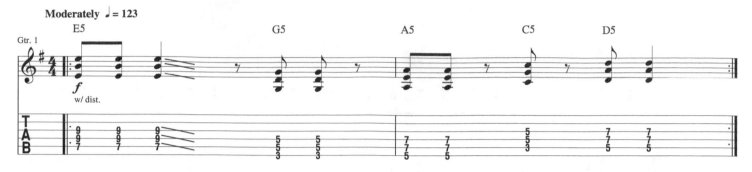

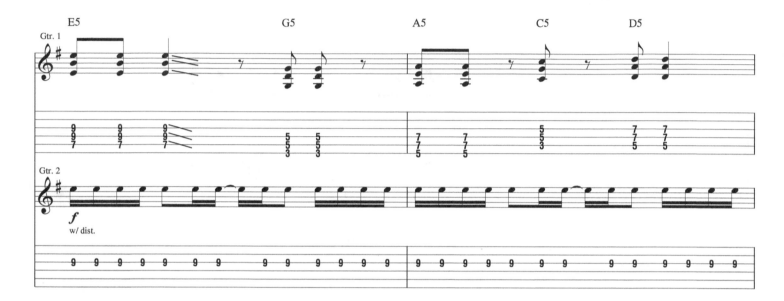

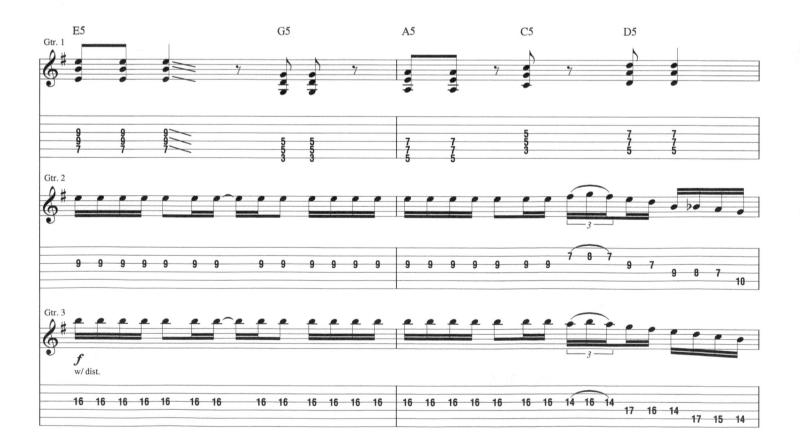

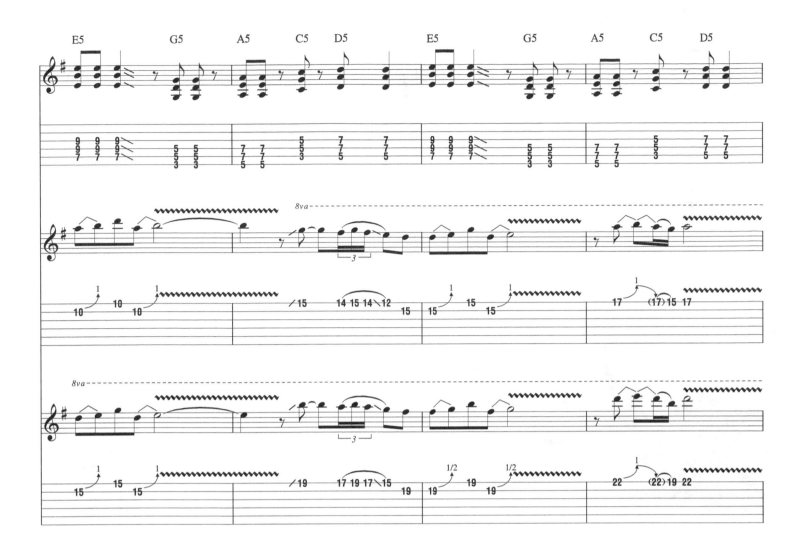

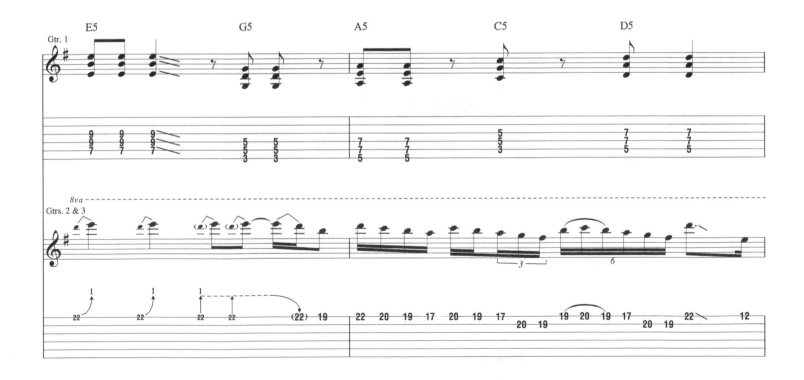

Artist: Scorpions

Album: *Love at First Sting*

Year: 1984

Guitarists: Rudolf Schenker, Matthias Jabs

Satellite
Words and Music by David J. Matthews

Artist: Dave Matthews Band

Album: *Under the Table and Dreaming*

Year: 1994

Guitarists: Dave Matthews, Tim Reynolds

Runnin' Down a Dream

Words and Music by Tom Petty, Jeff Lynne and Mike Campbell

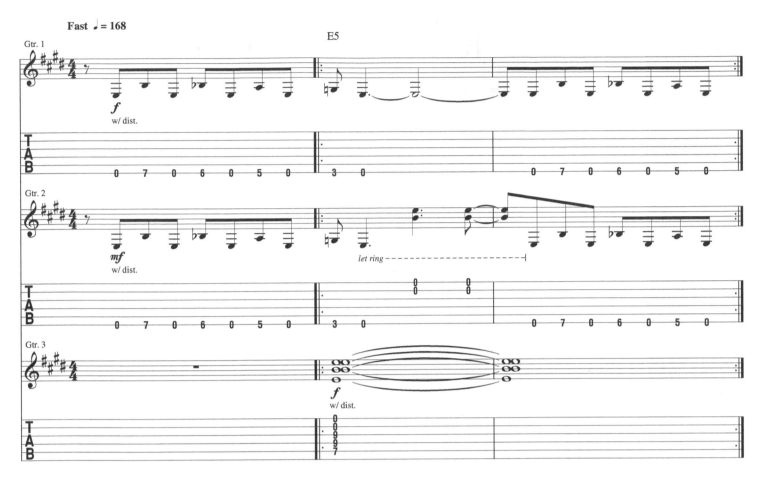

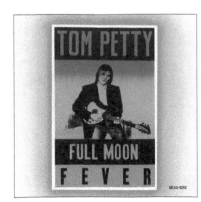

Artist: Tom Petty

Album: *Full Moon Fever*

Year: 1989

Guitarists: Tom Petty, Jeff Lynne, Mike Campbell

Roundabout

Words and Music by Jon Anderson and Steve Howe

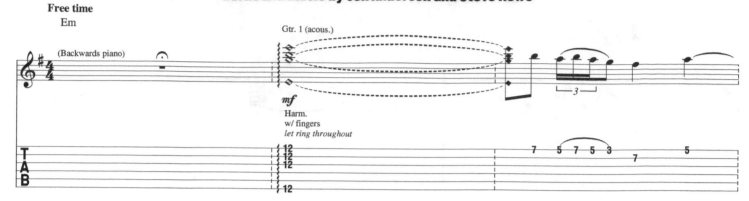

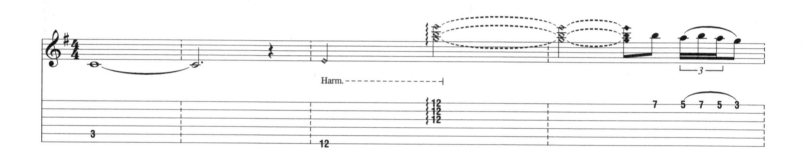

*Three gtrs. arr. for one.

Artist: Yes

Album: *Fragile*

Year: 1972

Guitarist: Steve Howe

Say It Ain't So

Words and Music by Rivers Cuomo

Tune down 1/2 step:
(low to high) Eb-Ab-Db-Gb-Bb-Eb

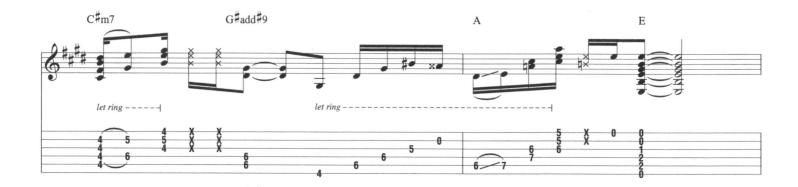

Artist: Weezer

Album: *Weezer* (blue album)

Year: 1994

Guitarists: Rivers Cuomo, Brian Bell

Secret Agent Man

from the Television Series
Words and Music by P.F. Sloan and Steve Barri

Artist: Johnny Rivers

Album: *...And I Know You Wanna Dance*

Year: 1966

Guitarist: Johnny Rivers

School's Out

Words and Music by Alice Cooper and Michael Bruce

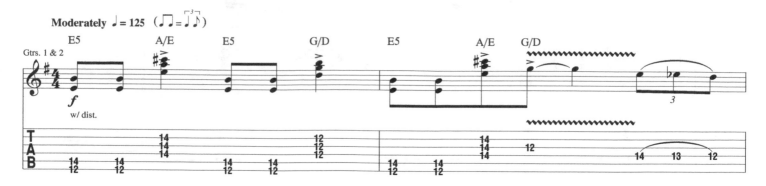

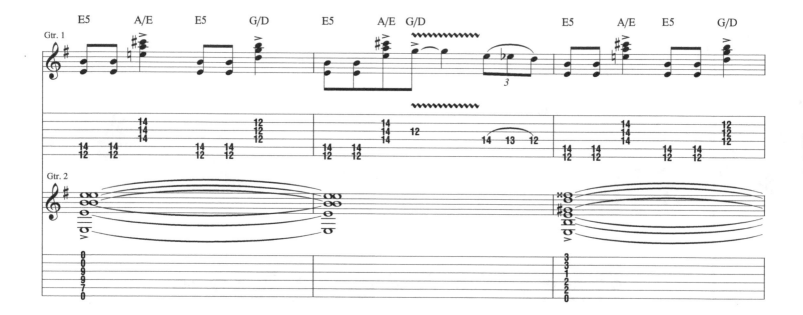

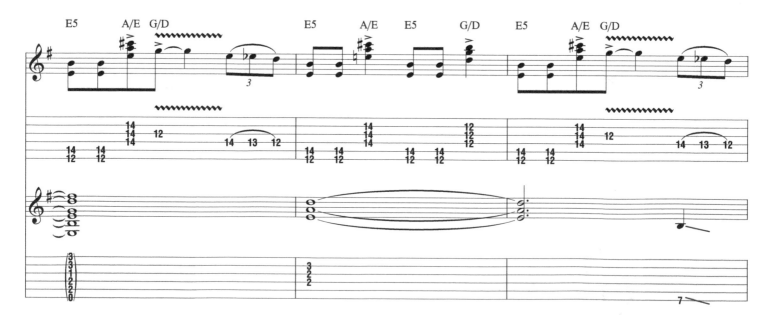

Artist: Alice Cooper

Album: *School's Out*

Year: 1972

Guitarists: Glen Buxton, Michael Bruce

Silent Lucidity

Words and Music by Chris DeGarmo

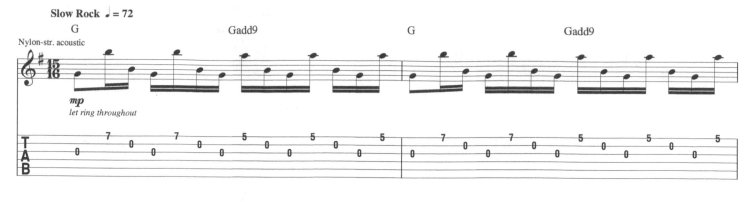

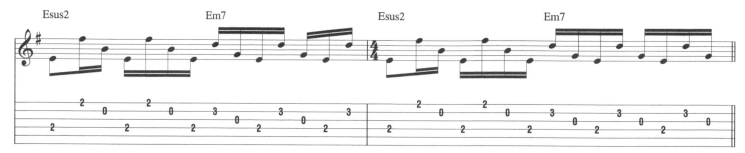

Artist: Queensrÿche

Album: *Empire*

Year: 1990

Guitarists: Chris DeGarmo, Michael Wilton

She Talks to Angels

Words and Music by Chris Robinson and Rich Robinson

Open D tuning, capo II:
(low to high) D-A-D-F#-A-D

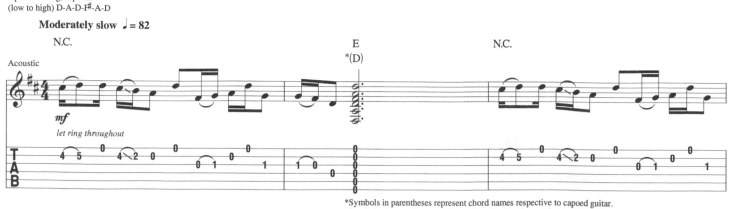

*Symbols in parentheses represent chord names respective to capoed guitar.
Symbols above reflect actual sounding chords. Capoed fret is "0" in tab.

Artist: The Black Crowes

Album: *Shake Your Money Maker*

Year: 1990

Guitarists: Rich Robinson, Jeff Cease

Seventeen

Words and Music by Kip Winger, Reb Beach and Beau Hill

Tune down 1/2 step:
(low to high) E♭-A♭-D♭-G♭-B♭-E♭

Moderate Rock ♩ = 96

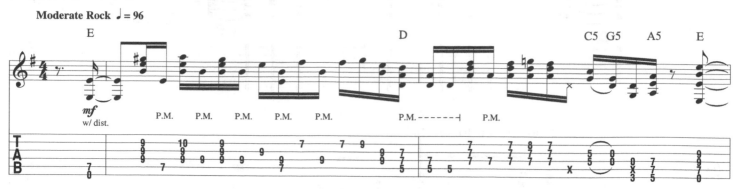

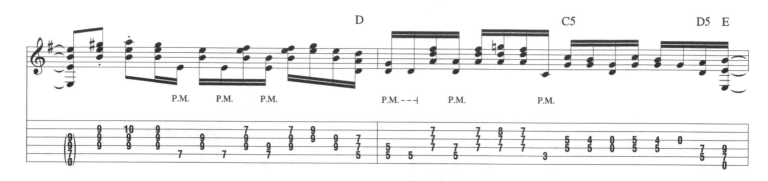

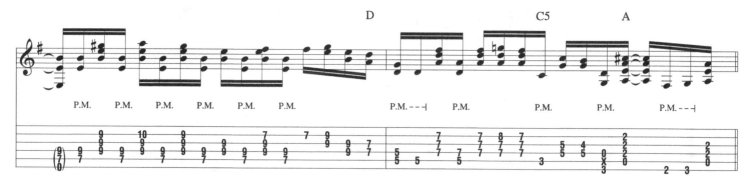

Artist: Winger

Album: *Winger*

Year: 1988

Guitarist: Reb Beach

Shine

Words and Music by Ed Roland

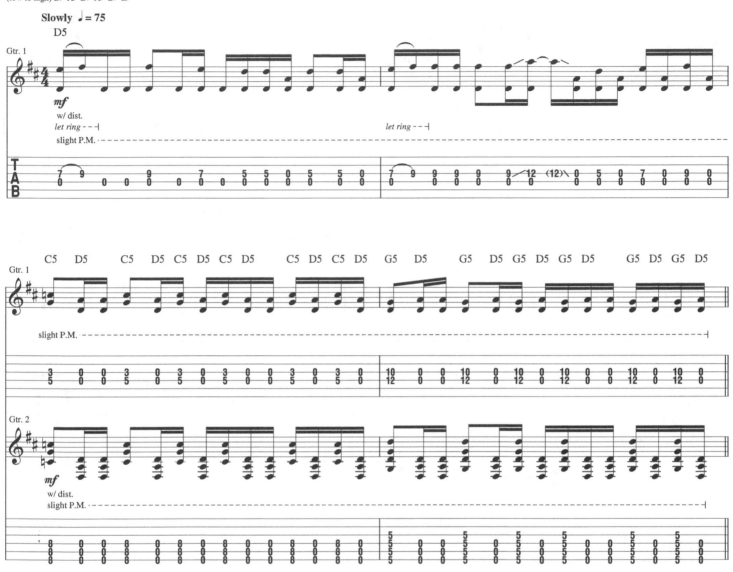

Artist: Collective Soul

Album: *Hints, Allegations and Things Left Unsaid*

Year: 1993

Guitarists: Dean Roland, Ross Childress

Smells Like Teen Spirit

Words and Music by Kurt Cobain, Krist Novoselic and Dave Grohl

Artist: Nirvana

Album: *Nevermind*

Year: 1991

Guitarist: Kurt Cobain

Smoke on the Water

Words and Music by Ritchie Blackmore, Ian Gillan, Roger Glover, Jon Lord and Ian Paice

Artist: Deep Purple

Album: *Machine Head*

Year: 1972

Guitarist: Ritchie Blackmore

Spoonman

Words and Music by Chris Cornell

Artist: Soundgarden

Album: *Superunknown*

Year: 1994

Guitarists: Kim Thayil, Chris Cornell

Soul Man

Words and Music by Isaac Hayes and David Porter

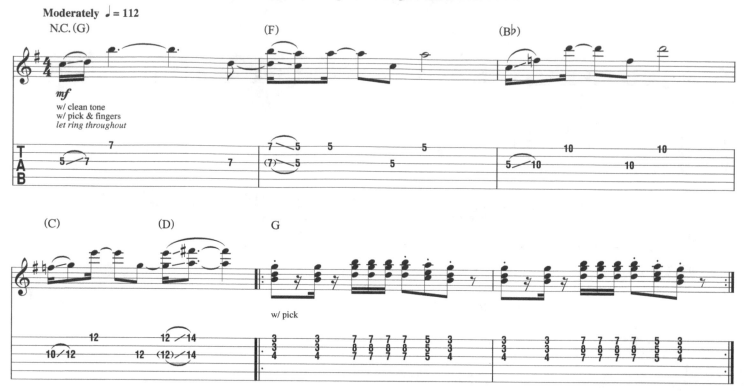

Artist: Sam & Dave

Album: *Soul Men*

Year: 1967

Guitarist: Steve Cropper

Stairway to Heaven

Words and Music by Jimmy Page and Robert Plant

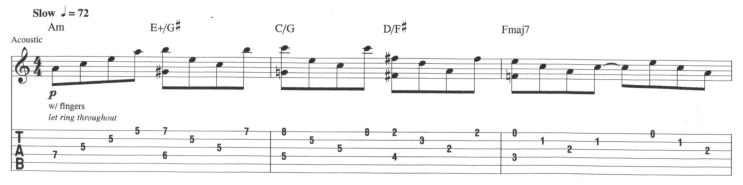

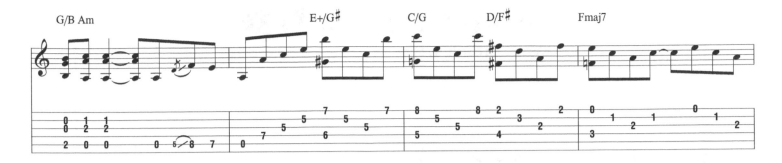

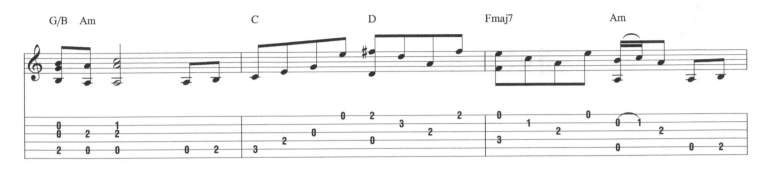

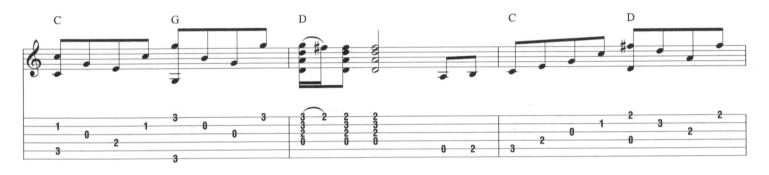

Artist: Led Zeppelin

Album: *Led Zeppelin IV*

Year: 1971

Guitarist: Jimmy Page

Start Me Up

Words and Music by Mick Jagger and Keith Richards

Gtr. 1: Open G tuning:
(low to high) D-G-D-G-B-D

Moderately ♩ = 124

*T = Thumb on 6th string

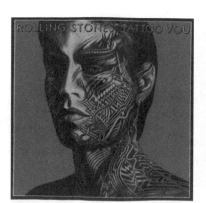

Artist: The Rolling Stones

Album: *Tattoo You*

Year: 1981

Guitarists: Keith Richards, Ron Wood

Sunshine of Your Love

Words and Music by Eric Clapton, Jack Bruce and Pete Brown

Moderately ♩ = 112

N.C.(D)

mf

w/ dist.

D   C D

C   D

Artist: Cream

Album: *Disraeli Gears*

Year: 1967

Guitarist: Eric Clapton

Sweet Child o' Mine

Words and Music by W. Axl Rose, Slash, Izzy Stradlin', Duff McKagan and Steven Adler

Tune down 1/2 step:
(low to high) Eb-Ab-Db-Gb-Bb-Eb

Moderately fast ♩ = 128

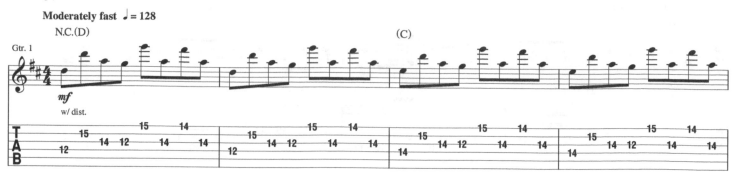

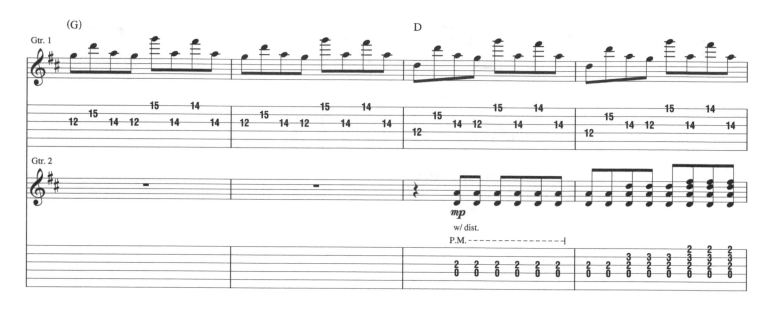

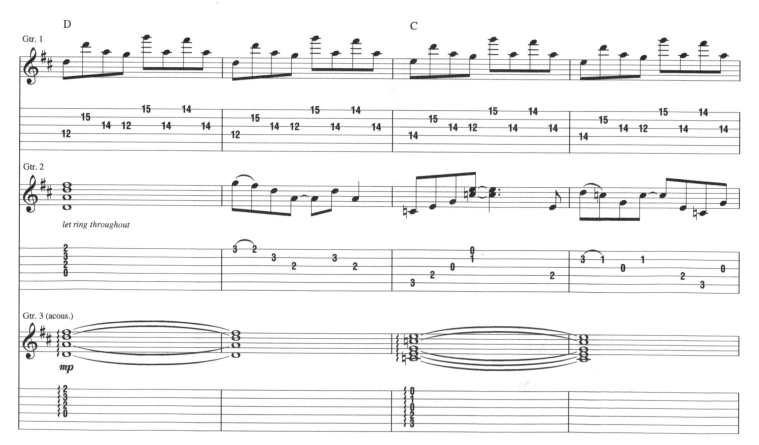

Artist: Guns N' Roses

Album: *Appetite for Destruction*

Year: 1987

Guitarists: Slash, Izzy Stradlin'

Sweet Home Alabama

Words and Music by Ronnie Van Zant, Ed King and Gary Rossington

*Key signature denotes D Mixolydian.

Artist: Lynyrd Skynyrd

Album: *Second Helping*

Year: 1974

Guitarists: Allen Collins, Gary Rossington, Ed King

Takin' Care of Business

Words and Music by Randy Bachman

*Key signature denotes C Mixolydian.

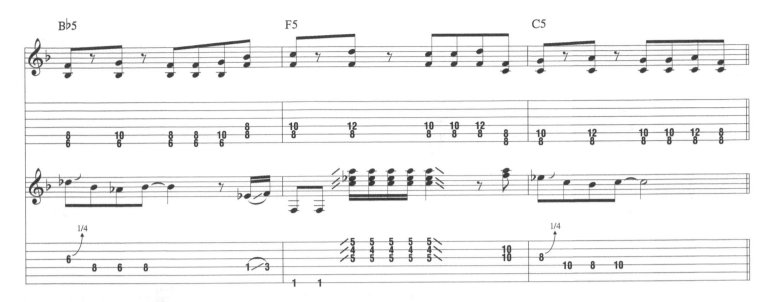

Artist: Bachman-Turner Overdrive

Album: *Bachman-Turner Overdrive II*

Year: 1973

Guitarists: Randy Bachman, Tim Bachman

The Trooper

Words and Music by Steven Harris

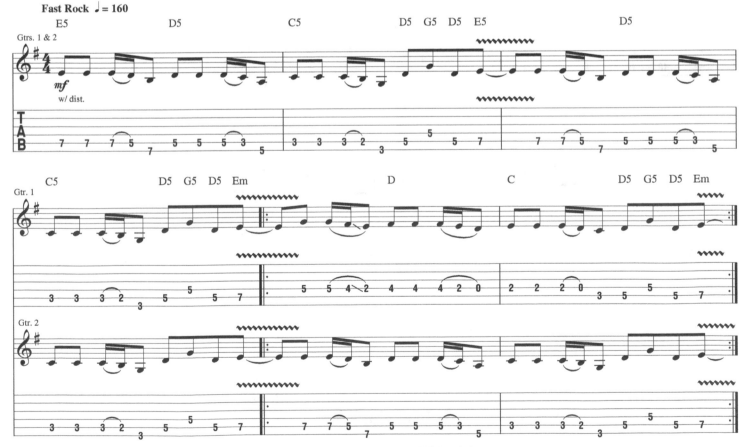

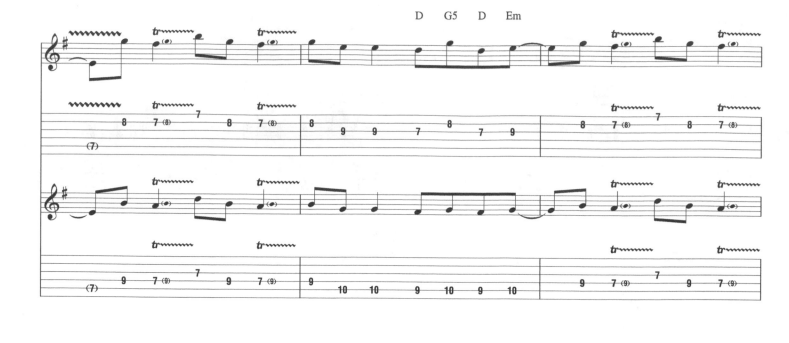

Artist: Iron Maiden

Album: *Piece of Mind*

Year: 1983

Guitarists: Dave Murray, Adrian Smith

Talk Dirty to Me

Words and Music by Bobby Dall, C.C. Deville, Bret Michaels and Rikki Rockett

Tune down 1/2 step:
(low to high) E♭-A♭-D♭-G♭-B♭-E♭

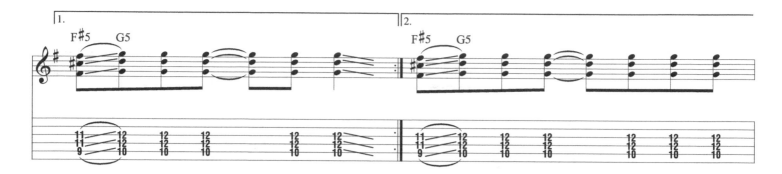

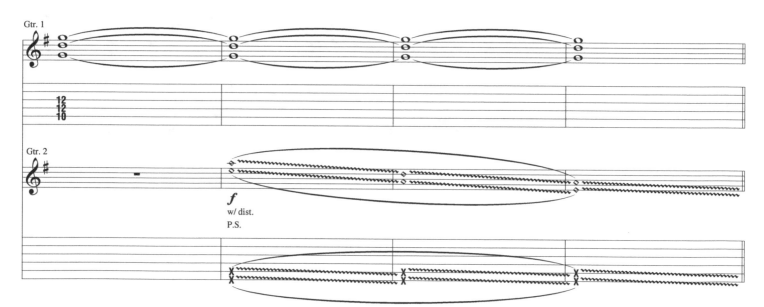

Artist: Poison

Album: *Look What the Cat Dragged In*

Year: 1986

Guitarist: C.C. DeVille

Tears in Heaven

Words and Music by Eric Clapton and Will Jennings

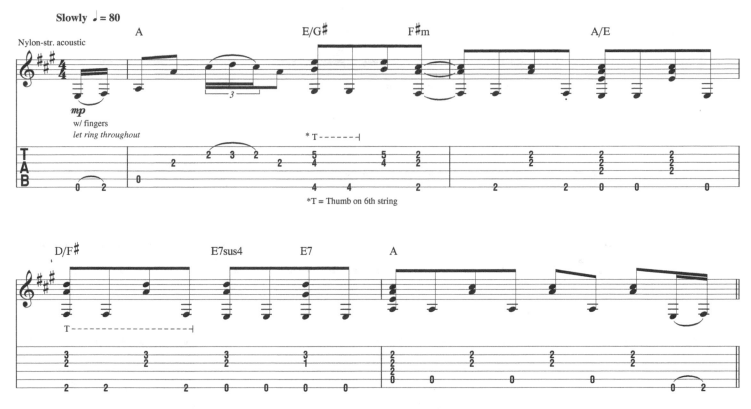

Artist: Eric Clapton

Album: *Unplugged*

Year: 1992

Guitarists: Eric Clapton, Andy Fairweather Low

Thunder Kiss '65

Words and Music by Rob Zombie, Sean Reynolds, Ivan de Prume and Jay Yuenger

Artist: White Zombie

Album: *La Sexorcisto: Devil Music, Vol. 1*

Year: 1992

Guitarist: J.

Thunderstruck

Words and Music by Angus Young and Malcolm Young

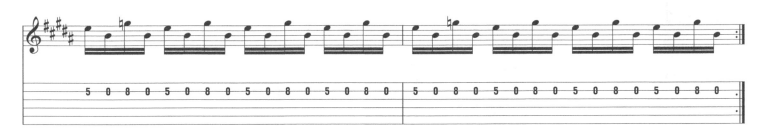

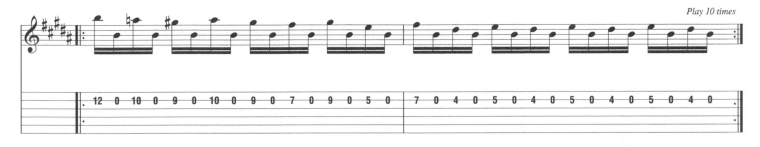

Artist: AC/DC

Album: *The Razor's Edge*

Year: 1990

Guitarists: Angus Young, Malcolm Young

Unchained

Words and Music by Edward Van Halen, Alex Van Halen, Michael Anthony and David Lee Roth

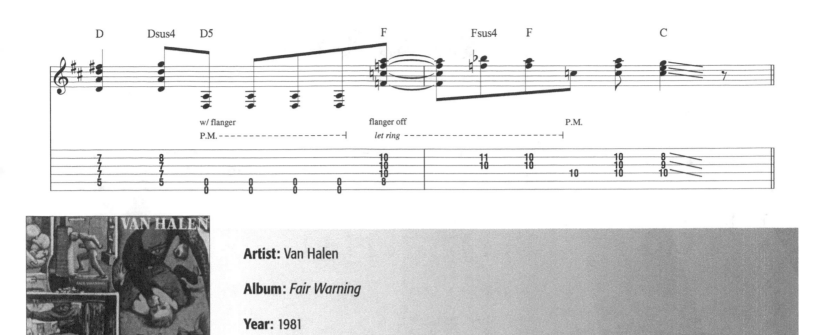

Artist: Van Halen

Album: *Fair Warning*

Year: 1981

Guitarist: Edward Van Halen

Up Around the Bend

Words and Music by John Fogerty

Artist: Creedence Clearwater Revival

Album: *Cosmo's Factory*

Year: 1970

Guitarists: John Fogerty, Tom Fogerty

25 or 6 to 4

Words and Music by Robert Lamm

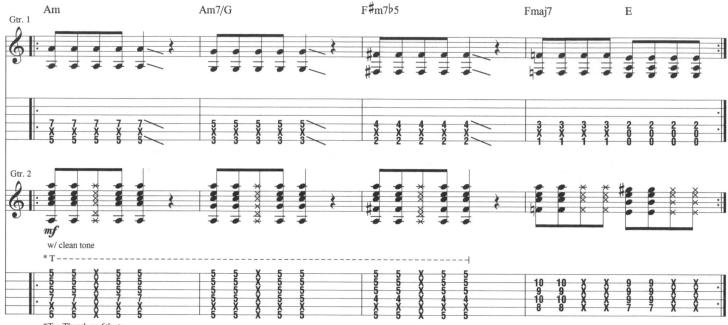

*T = Thumb on 6th str.

Artist: Chicago

Album: *Chicago*

Year: 1970

Guitarist: Terry Kath

Wake Up Little Susie

Words and Music by Boudleaux Bryant and Felice Bryant

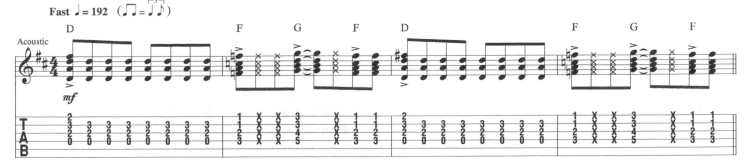

Fast ♩ = 192

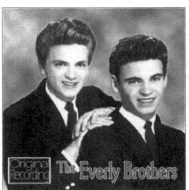

Artist: The Everly Brothers

Album: *The Everly Brothers*

Year: 1958

Guitarists: Don Everly, Phil Everly

Walk This Way

Words and Music by Steven Tyler and Joe Perry

Moderately ♩ = 120

N.C.(E5)

Artist: Aerosmith

Album: *Toys in the Attic*

Year: 1975

Guitarists: Joe Perry, Brad Whitford

Voodoo Child (Slight Return)

Words and Music by Jimi Hendrix

Tune down 1/2 step:
(low to high) Eb-Ab-Db-Gb-Bb-Eb

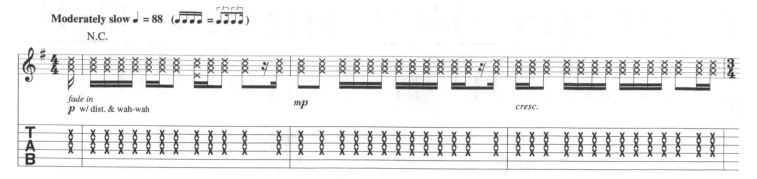

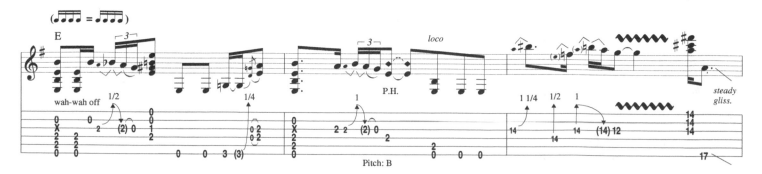

* Flick pickup selector between neck and middle pickups.

Fuzz Face off

8va   loco   8va   loco

P.H.   P.H.

Pitch: B   Pitch: B

Artist: The Jimi Hendrix Experience

Album: *Electric Ladyland*

Year: 1968

Guitarist: Jimi Hendrix

Wheel in the Sky

Words and Music by Robert Fleischman, Neal Schon and Diane Valory

Artist: Journey

Album: *Infinity*

Year: 1978

Guitarist: Neal Schon

Wanted Dead or Alive

Words and Music by Jon Bon Jovi and Richie Sambora

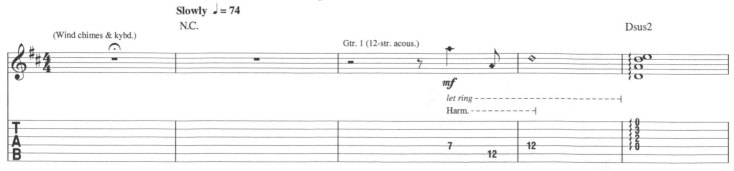

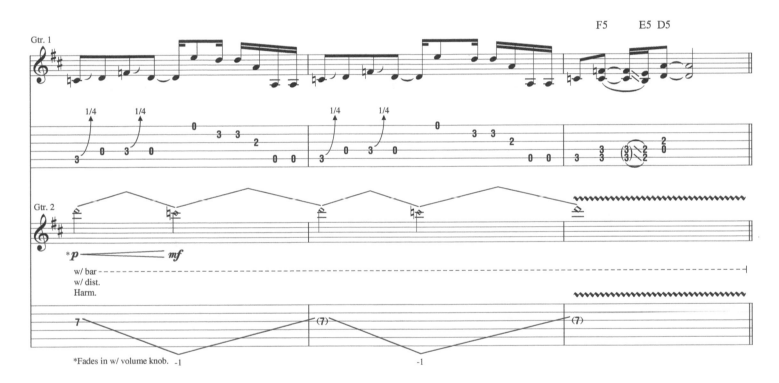

Artist: Bon Jovi

Album: *Slippery When Wet*

Year: 1986

Guitarist: Richie Sambora

Wish You Were Here

Words and Music by Roger Waters and David Gilmour

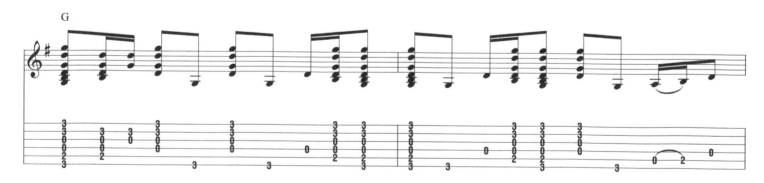

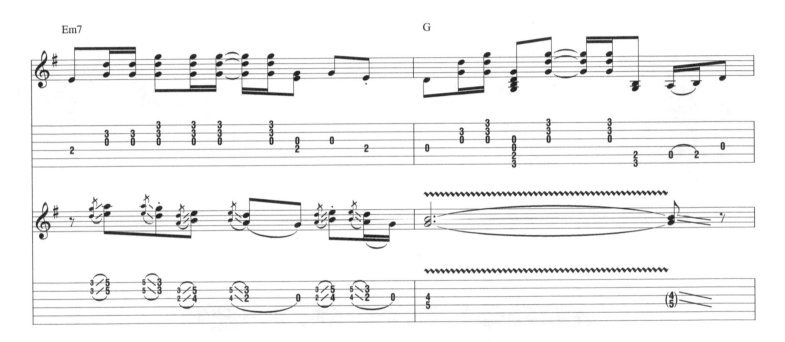

Artist: Pink Floyd

Album: *Wish You Were Here*

Year: 1975

Guitarist: David Gilmour

Under the Bridge

Words and Music by Anthony Kiedis, Flea, John Frusciante and Chad Smith

Artist: Red Hot Chili Peppers

Album: *Blood Sugar Sex Magik*

Year: 1991

Guitarist: John Frusciante

Walk

Words and Music by Vince Abbott, Darrell Abbott, Rex Brown and Phil Anselmo

*Tune down 1 step:
(low to high) D-G-C-F-A-D

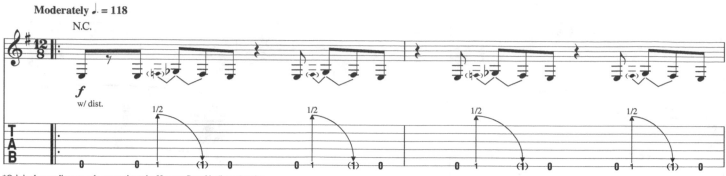

*Original recording sounds approximately 60 cents flat of indicated tuning.

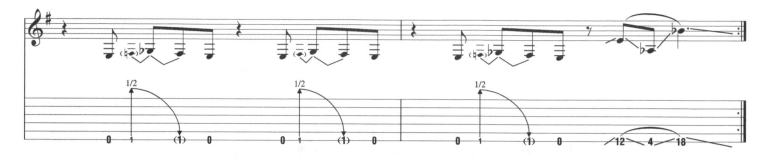

Artist: Pantera

Album: *Vulgar Display of Power*

Year: 1992

Guitarist: Dimebag Darrell

You Really Got Me

Words and Music by Ray Davies

Tune down 1/2 step:
(low to high) Eb-Ab-Db-Gb-Bb-Eb

Moderately fast ♩ = 140

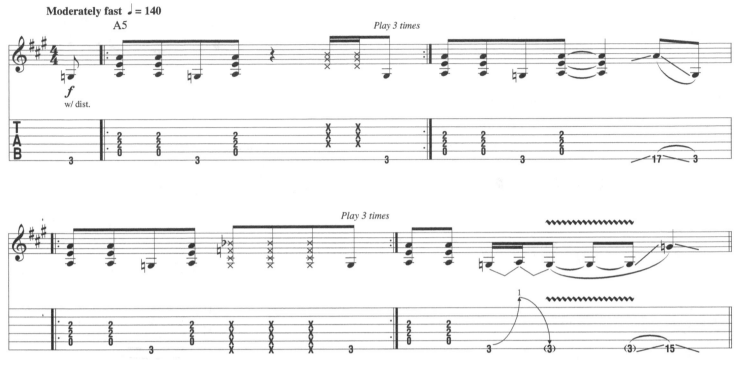

Artist: Van Halen

Album: *Van Halen*

Year: 1978

Guitarist: Edward Van Halen

You Shook Me All Night Long

Words and Music by Angus Young, Malcolm Young and Brian Johnson

Artist: AC/DC

Album: *Back in Black*

Year: 1980

Guitarists: Angus Young, Malcolm Young